Ken Kalb

Let's Turn on
The Light of the World

— PUBLISHED BY LUCKY STAR PRESS —

Box 5796
SANTA BARBARA, CA 93150

Copyright 1998
by KEN KALB

www.lightshift.com
Library of Congress Catalog Card Number
97-09283778382

ISBN 0-9642927-7-7

Printed in the United States of America
All rights reserved
12345678910

100% recycled paper

OTHER BOOKS BY KEN KALB

LOVE SONG FOR A MYSTERIOUS PLANET (1982)

THE GRAND CATHARSIS (1994)

THE GRAND CATHARSIS (1996)
(Revised edition)

KEN KALB is also the author of hundreds of magazine articles, an eloquent lecturer and workshop leader, a renowned astrologer and healer, coordinator of numerous transformational projects, and a dedicated seeker of truth and lover of life.

ACKNOWLEDGEMENTS

Abundant blessings to
Annette Berlin for her graphic design and layout,
Oceanna for her beautiful illustrations,
Bo von Hoenlohe for his webmastering on the LightShift site
Da Vid for his indefatigable networking and wisdom,
and all of the wonderful people coming together in radiance and
grand intention to help bring the human community
closer together.

This is dedicated to the

Humankind

GOD

Mother Earth

ONE I LOVE

CONTENTS

The Four Horseman of the Apocalypse—Famine, War, Pestilence, and Death—will gallop furiously across the face of the Earth, according to a growing cadre of sensationalists peddling their special brand of millennial madness. The sale of fear in bizarre forms is a huge and lucrative industry, and this mythic divide provides a fertile marketplace for doomsayers and alarmists to suck you in. On most nights, a popular radio or TV program features a maven with an astonishing version of how it's all going to come tumbling down: Pole shifts, colliding asteroids, viruses from outer space, appearances of antichrists, biblical prophecy of apocalypse, photon bands, secrets from the Great Sphinx, reports from the Dead Sea Scrolls, messages from disembodied souls, strange UFO and ET scenarios, new takes on Nostradamus and Cayce, and other brands of end-time hysteria. Each sounds convincing, and each has something to sell.

Yet it won't happen quite like any of this. "Don't worry, be happy," said Meher Baba. We are creating our future every moment. Our fate has yet to be written or sealed.

At the same time, I cannot deny that Durer's horsemen do indeed ride high, though in different fashion than most prognosticator's proselytize. Sanity and truth are becoming rare and valuable commodities in this day and age. Yet we do indeed live in a truly momentus time; a time akin to the people who lived during the birth of Christ.

Wouldn't it be wonderful if our brilliant scientists using our advanced technology could build a world peace machine, an environmental cleanup and balancing apparatus, a global disease prevention instrument, or a planetary hunger eliminator? Wouldn't it be awesome if the leaders of nations united in a vision of unity and wholeness for peace, health, and happiness on Earth, and implemented their vision using these tools. And wouldn't it be great if the leaders of business and industry came together and operated from their hearts instead of their pocketbooks?

The solution to world peace and most other 21st century human problems, however, is a spiritual solution, not a technological panacea. Surely technology will play a fundamental role. But as the French existentialist Andre Malraux once said, **"the third millennium will be spiritual, or it will not be."**

So I bring good news and bad news in this regard.

First, the bad news. No mechanistic technology and no amount of money alone will solve these problems. Nor does it appear that any global leader or influential individual or group (though I would love to be wrong) has the vision, the desire, or the compassion to initiate the radical action needed to transform our problems into solutions.

Now, the good news. I know of a technology, which can literally create miracles. God has given us all the instructions on how to create it. In fact, it is presently under construction. It is indeed all of the above mentioned devices in one. And **you** are a fundamental part of the system.

The human being is itself, the most extraordinary technology in the universe. Each of us is equipped with a spiritual power which when activated in its purity and clarity, is capable of manifesting miracles. When we join together in silence from our divine light with grand intention, we synergize and multiply this ability. And when millions of people synchronistically merge in a shared vision of wholeness, such a powerful surge of light floods and amplifies the unified field of human consciousness, that miracles fertilize and activate through the collective Mind and Heart of humankind. This is the LightShift—the hope of the future. The awesome light and love of the collective Heart of humanity will empower and assist all of the other inspired efforts centering on the year 2000 and the millennial year (2000-2001) as a turning point in the direction of civilization.

When Marianne Williamson asked if mass meditation could save the world, the Dalai Lama replied, **"if we wish to save the world, we must have a plan, but unless we meditate, no plan will work."** A profusion of plans are forming around the millennium as a springboard for upgrading the quality of human life. We wish to fertilize the unified field of collective consciousness with radiance and love, like a farmer feeds healthy soil, to yield a golden harvest.

The brilliance of mind, the beauty in our hearts, and the divinity of our spirits has equipped us with everything we need to turn the course of civilization around in a more positive direction. The true **"pole shift"** is a radical adjustment in our values and priorities. The new millennium is the time for this turnaround. If we get our minds and hearts aligned, everything else will fall into place.

Here are eight of the fundamental adjustments:

- We must acknowledge our problems fully.
- We must think in terms of **We**, instead of just **Me**.
- Humanity must consider itself a global family, working and playing in unity in our diversity and harmony in our variety.

- Business leaders and corporations must open their hearts and practice compassionate capitalism, where the prime directive of increasing wealth equally considers enhancing the quality of life and maintaining our delicate and vital balances.
- We must elect and empower enlightened spiritual leaders who use **their** bully pulpit and **our** vast resources to invigorate inspirational programs to meet and beat our challenges.
- Our collective will, imagination, and passion must be ignited so we are inspired to spring into action.
- We must live with a golden rule mentality where we treat others and Mother Gaia as we would like to be treated ourselves.
- We must all dig a little deeper and shine a little brighter.

Let's consider this exemplary point for a moment. There are now over 500 billionaires on Earth whose net worth is equivalent to the entire lower half of the world's population. That's right, 500 Earthlings are worth the same as 3,000,000,000 fellow humans! The United Nations Human Development report of 1997 estimated that the money needed to end planetary poverty was $80 billion over the next ten years—less than the combined net worth of the seven richest men in the world. With the exception of Ted Turner, who committed $1 billion to the United Nations—The Sultan of Brunei, Bill Gates and the rest of the 500 club are primarily busy widening the gap. Consider what incredible good could be done with all the revenue of the tax deductions of these 500 billionaires and other wealthy individuals and corporations invested in a compassionate superfund!

When we set our collective will toward a goal, we are capable of imagineering what seems impossible. We have done this many times before. Here are two examples from history.

In 1960, President John F. Kennedy announced that in a decade we would land a man on the Moon, initiating the **Space Race**. On July 20, 1969, the Eagle landed, marking "one great step for man, and one huge leap for mankind."

During World War II, the decision was made to develop a weapon, so powerful in its destructive capability, that it would immediately defeat the enemy and end any further fighting. A directive known as the **Manhattan Project** was initiated allocating virtually unlimited funds and assembling an all-star team of our greatest scientists, physicists, engineers, designers, and builders to create the atomic bomb in the quickest time. The exigency of the emergency mentality fueling the project resulted in the creation of a doomsday device from a theoretical concept by August 8, 1945, when the US dropped the atomic bomb on Hiroshima.

Now, in the current relative military peace on our planet, we find ourselves in a different type of global conflict, in many ways far more insidious than the previous two, for it threatens our very survival as a species. One might consider that humankind is in a silent, yet deadly Third World War, declared on ourselves through growing overpopulation and unbridled greed. This has taken the form of overproduction and consumption, resulting in the deterioration and destruction of our environment and quality of life. We forgot that "we do not inherit the land from our ancestors, we borrow it from our children." And it may indeed simply be our children's incredible will to live which creates our future.

Since we have waged this war on ourselves, it is also up to us to declare our **truce**, and establish our **peace**.

Disregarding decades of warnings for zero population growth, Earth's population is approaching 6 billion, and expected to double by 2050. Population and progress has had the side effect of making Mother Earth ill, challenging her fragile and balanced ecosystems. The late Jacques Cousteau insisted our seas are on their deathbed, with the plankton and phytoplankton at the foundation of the food chain dying. Our tropical rain forests, the very lungs of our planet, are being eviscerated at a rate which could see them disappear imminently. The UN says that two thirds of humanity will lack clean fresh water by 2027, about the same time The Earth runs out of crude oil. Civilization's waste gases are destabilizing the atmosphere, and most scientists now concur the planet is warming while the ozone layer is depleting to near cataclysmic levels. I could go on and on, but you are aware of this story, which is not a pretty picture.

Despite global conferences in Rio, Europe, and Kyoto, only small measures are being initiated to grapple with our plethora of environmental problems. **Big problems need powerful solutions.** Though the very survival of humankind is at stake, we certainly have no *Manhattan Project* or *Space Race* mentality for surmounting these monumental millennial challenges. Though I certainly hope our collective LightShift energy will feed the extra juice to assist the United Nations labors in developing a mighty and enforceable environmental Earth Charter by the year 2000, as well as the hundreds of other inspired activities focusing on the millennium as a turning point toward a brighter future.

For the mystical, mythical, and magical date of the year 2000 serves as an ignition point for the great hope of humanity coming together as one united family, beaming peacefully and radiantly with grand intention. We have the opportunity amidst overwhelming obstacles to make a turnaround from one of the most destructive periods in history, to a new era focused on a brighter vision of peace, cooperation, sustainability, and unity for all. Hundreds of thousands of men, women, and children are already joining in the LightShift first of each month at Noon meditations and prayers all over the world. Hundreds of inspired projects are focusing on the year 2000 as a birthing point for a turnaround. Like a caterpillar in chrysalis transforming into a butterfly, a radiant energy surrounds the birth of the third millennium. There is fresh hope we will see our children's sparkling eyes greeting the new dawn.

A baseball analogy may be appropriate. It's 6 to nothing with two outs in the bottom of the 9th inning, with Darth Vader on the mound for the dark side. Things are looking pretty grim for the people of planet Earth, when suddenly, the crowd goes wild as...Yoda...comes to bat! May the force be with us as we swing into action to manifest a millennial miracle.

"You may say I'm a Dreamer, but I'm not the only one. I hope someday you'll join us: And the World will be as One."
—John Lennon

"Never doubt that a small group of thoughtful, committed citizens can change the world. Indeed it is the only thing that ever has!"
—Margaret Mead

THE PROJECT

Imagine millions of men, women and children
merged in the same beautiful spirit

May we join together...
in a synchronized universal meditation
to raise the consciousness of all humanity

May we affirm...
to live a brighter new vision that all life can share
May we visualize...
a thousand years of peace on Earth
starting with this moment

May we embrace...
all people—whatever race, religion, non-religion,
beliefs, or nationality
May we remember...
In the Heart there is no division

only Oneness in Spirit
We are All Children of God in the Family of Human

May the Beauty in our Hearts
the Brilliance of our Minds
and the Divinity of our Spirits,
Create this new Vision

May Love and Light fill our lives
and change our World...
and from this Great Spirit
May we come together to brighten the future

On January 1, 1999 ◆ 2000 ◆ 2001
We Will Turn on the Light of the World!

THE VISION

At 11:59 PM on December 31st of 1999, all of the calendric cycles of day, month, year, decade, century, and millennium will shift in a hopeful moment. The energy of a thousand New Year's Eves will be amplified in the hearts and minds of all the peoples of planet Earth. A rare opportunity presents itself for humanity to band together in the quantum numbers necessary to create a powerful circuit of light to greet the dawn of the new millennium.* We feel that this unified circuit has the potential of shifting the collective consciousness to a higher octave and transforming the course of history in a more positive direction.

We invite you to be part of this radiant millennial moment—hopefully, the most powerful and positive shift in human history. And we encourage and welcome any and all groups with a similar vision to lay aside little differences, and join together in this effort. For together, **we are the LightShift...and the hope of the future.**

*See page 66, "The Millenium Quirk"

You read these words now for good reason. You are hereby empowered as a spiritual revolutionary and an agent of positive change which we call The LightShift. Your mission is most possible: On the First day of next month at Noon, and at Noon on the First of each month thereafter, please join us in silent meditation for 15 minutes from the pure light within. You thus become a radiant thread in the tapestry we are weaving around this planet which will be fully woven by January 1, 2000—**One Day In Peace.**

We live in a time of massive and countless imbalances and challenges on all levels, which literally threaten our survival as a civilization and as a species. The new millennium is a razor's edge in time where we either rise above the past or become victims to it. The latter is not a viable option. We all wish to see our children's sparkling eyes smiling at the Sun.

Meditation is of great benefit both for us as individuals and for the quality of the collective consciousness. Hundreds of city, state, and national studies have been published in scientific journals concluding that when just 1% of the population is meditating, the quality of life improves for everyone. Furthermore, crime, violence, illness, and all the other byproducts of accumulated social stress decrease. The influence of mass meditations on collective consciousness and life is profound, and the simplest and singular most powerful thing we can do to positively impact the present, *and* the future.

As a famous Indian sage once said, **"if just one tenth of one percent of humanity were focused together in transcendental consciousness, it would create the pilot light to ignite the divinity in all humanity."** This is precisely the intention of LightShift 2000.

As the labyrinth of the LightShift logo depicts, we are all connected on the **"innernet."** Within this unity of heart and spirit focused on the pure light within, we will create massive waves of love and compassion, raising the consciousness of all humanity, to usher in this new millennium in the sweetest and brightest light. Your participation is essential to our success.

—Hiiaka—

THE PLAN

♦ The Buildup—Creating a Wave of Light

Starting with the first day of the next month, please take 15 minutes to meditate on the pure light within you at Noon. Please Continue this on the first day of every month thereafter until the big events on January 1, 1999, 2000, and 2001 at Midnight. Many people are also meditating at Noon and 7PM on Sundays.

♦ New Year's 1999 ♦ 2000 ♦ 2001 ♦ Celebrate—Meditate—Celebrate!

The natural inclination for most people on a New Year's Eve is to hug, kiss, holler, drum, release energy, set off fireworks, etc. So we say, celebrate...then meditate...then celebrate!

After your celebration, let us proceed at 12:12 AM (some may wish to start at midnight, others a bit later than 12:12) into a silent meditation on the pure light within until 1 AM. You may wish to light a candle or a fire as a symbol of this ignition of new light. If you are part of a meditation or spiritual group, let us all link together for this endeavor. If not, you can simply do it yourself! It doesn't matter where you are. Simple universal meditation instructions are given in chapter 6 for those who don't already know how. After your meditation, let's celebrate with music and joy throughout the world!

♦ What about the different time zones?

So many people will be participating that it isn't necessary to synchronize the time zones around the planet. We feel this will create beautiful "waves of consciousness" before, during, and after Midnight in your locale throughout the entire planet.

♦ Keep it Alive: Let's Meditate the First Day of Every Month at Noon

Those of you who have participated in large meditations such as

Harmonic Convergence or GaiaMind know what a wonderful experience this is. Ideally, we should carry this feeling and spirit forth into every moment of our lives.

At Noon on the First of each Month through January 1st of 2001, let's meditate again for fifteen minutes. This will sustain and maintain this elevation of consciousness, lighting the way into the new millennium—fertilizing the unified field of collective consciousness in radiance to help empower all of the wonderful endeavors which are being initiated.

◆ Let's Do Something Every Day!

We acknowledge the efforts of the **World Peace Prayer Society** who is devoted exclusively to spreading the affirmation, **"May Peace Prevail on Earth,"** and invite you to consider saying this prayer at Noon every day.

◆ Spread the Word!

If you are on the internet, we invite you to visit the LightShift website at **www.lightshift.com.** There are buttons for making flyers, which you can email, fax, photocopy, or mail to everyone you know and love. If not, please network this information in any way you can. If you have any media contacts or creative ideas for spreading the word, please let us know. For you are as much the LightShift as we.

Hundreds of thousands of people are already participating in the monthly meditations. Thousands of lamas high up in the Himalayas are synchronizing with the LightShift meditations. We have even initiated an effort to invite the two million inmates, incarcerated in America's prisons, who have little more than an inner life, to participate in the LightShift meditations. The response has been enthusiastic and ecstatic.

Dear friend, YOU are the LightShift: It was created for you to make your own. You and me, and everyone we know and contact—coming together in peace and light. We…are the hope of the future. Together we will make the difference….for in our alignment during this radiant millennial moment…is the promise of grand fulfillment.

COMMON bE YOUR pRAYER;
COMMON bE YOUR qOAl;
COMMON bE YOUR puRposE;
COMMON bE YOUR delibERATiON
COMMON bE YOUR wisHES,
YOUR HEARTS iN CONcoRd,
YOUR iNTENTiONS iN CONcoRd,
PERfEcT bE tHE uNiON AMONq YOU.
—**Riq VEdA**

J A N U A R Y   1 ,   1 9 9 9   ◆   1 1 1 9 9 9
A L P H A   A N D   O M E G A

The first day of the last year of the bimillennium, January 1, 1999, exhibits a unique configuration of numbers with powerful metaphysical significance. The number One represents unity, and the beginning or alpha portion of a cycle, while the number Nine represents the omega, end, or eternal phase. As every ending births a new beginning, January 1, 1999 is both alpha and omega, marking the commencement of the end of a two thousand year calendric cycle—a completion *and* an initiation.

January 1, 1999 adds up numerologically to the magical number three, represented by the triangle or trinity. The triangle symbolizes perfection: Pointing upward it means the spiritual ascent to heaven or higher consciousness, fire, and the active male principle. Reversed, it symbolizes water, the passive feminine principle, and the bringer of all earthly manifestation. Notice also how the one's and nine's of this rare date are grouped in two sets of three's or trinity's. There are numerous triune cycles: The 3, 6, 9 relationship of the ancient Chinese oracle, the I Ching, the three levels of mind (subconscious, conscious, and superconscious), the three primary colors, the three components of being (body, mind and spirit), the Holy Trinity of the bible (the Father, the Son, and the Holy Ghost), or the Planetary Trinity of Humankind, Mother Earth, and God. Trinitization is also dynamically embodied in the three dimensional form of the star tetrahedron or Merkaba—representing the light/spirit/body in energetic activation. This universal principle of trinitization embodies completion and perfection within itself. All of these components target this date, 1/1/1999, as a time to reflect on our completion of this old cycle, and prepare for our metamorphosis into the next evolutionary phase. This is also why January 1, 1999 will be the time of the first of the three LightShift 2000 quantum meditations, bridging the millennial years, 1999—2001.

"A ʜᴜᴍᴀɴ ʙᴇⁱɴɢ ⁱs ᴘᴀʀᴛ ᴏf ᴀ wʜᴏʟᴇ, ᴄᴀʟʟᴇᴅ ʙʏ ᴜs ᴛʜᴇ "Uɴⁱᴠᴇʀsᴇ," ᴀ ᴘᴀʀᴛ ʟⁱᴍⁱᴛᴇᴅ ⁱɴ ᴛⁱᴍᴇ ᴀɴᴅ sᴘᴀᴄᴇ. Hᴇ ᴇxᴘᴇʀⁱᴇɴᴄᴇs ʜⁱᴍsᴇʟf, ʜⁱs ᴛʜᴏᴜɢʜᴛs ᴀɴᴅ fᴇᴇʟⁱɴɢs, ᴀs sᴏᴍᴇᴛʜⁱɴɢ sᴇᴘᴀʀᴀᴛᴇᴅ fʀᴏᴍ ᴛʜᴇ ʀᴇsᴛ ᴀ ᴋⁱɴᴅ ᴏf ᴏᴘᴛⁱᴄᴀʟ ᴅᴇʟᴜsⁱᴏɴ ᴏf ᴄᴏɴsᴄⁱᴏᴜsɴᴇss. Tʜⁱs ᴅᴇʟᴜsⁱᴏɴ ⁱs ᴀ ᴋⁱɴᴅ ᴏf ᴘʀⁱsᴏɴ fᴏʀ ᴜs, ʀᴇsᴛʀⁱᴄᴛⁱɴɢ ᴜs ᴛᴏ ᴏᴜʀ ᴘᴇʀsᴏɴᴀʟ ᴅᴇsⁱʀᴇs ᴀɴᴅ ᴛᴏ ᴀffᴇᴄᴛⁱᴏɴ fᴏʀ ᴀ fᴇw ᴘᴇʀsᴏɴs ɴᴇᴀʀᴇsᴛ ᴜs. Oᴜʀ ᴛᴀsᴋ ᴍᴜsᴛ ʙᴇ ᴛᴏ fʀᴇᴇ ᴏᴜʀsᴇʟᴠᴇs fʀᴏᴍ ᴛʜⁱs ᴘʀⁱsᴏɴ ʙʏ wⁱᴅᴇɴⁱɴɢ ᴏᴜʀ ᴄⁱʀᴄʟᴇs ᴏf ᴄᴏᴍᴘᴀssⁱᴏɴ ᴛᴏ ᴇᴍʙʀᴀᴄᴇ ᴀʟʟ ʟⁱᴠⁱɴɢ ᴄʀᴇᴀᴛᴜʀᴇs ᴀɴᴅ ᴛʜᴇ wʜᴏʟᴇ ᴏf ɴᴀᴛᴜʀᴇ ⁱɴ ⁱᴛs ʙᴇᴀᴜᴛʏ."
—Aʟʙᴇʀᴛ Eⁱɴsᴛᴇⁱɴ

Tʜᴇ Lⁱɢʜᴛ Sʜⁱfᴛ

LightShift is a spiritual revolution. It is a call from spirit, by spirit, and for spirit to unite in our silence and our light with grand intention. We believe that this is the singular most powerful thing we can do to boost the frequency on this planet to raise the light quotient to the point of critical mass awakening. We also feel this surge will permeate into all areas of life and positively impact the course of civilization on Earth.

In essence, spirit is energy which manifests as light. As we evolve, we become more light and less dense. Powerful waves of awakening are now surging on Earth as our natural evolution and spiritual destiny. The more light each of us can anchor, the more good we can do for each other and our planet. Banding together in this elevated frequency, we create a circuit whose resonance can create miracles. By synchronizing a quantum number of beings in this spirit, we concentrate our intensity and form the radiant core from which a mass illumination ignites. For this is indeed the manifestation of the Aquarian Christ—blazing through each of our hearts as **One**.

May all Lightworkers now unite to cocreate our future!

For it is only in alignment that there can be fulfillment—only in unity where we cocreate manifestation. Though there may be great diversity in our lives, we all share a divine spark, a luminous core of light from the great Heart of God. Around this core, may we find the unity in our diversity, and the harmony in our variety to rally for this noble purpose.

Can consciousness change the course of history? Most certainly! If we expand or elevate our own consciousness, our life changes; look at the incredible transformation of Baba RamDass from Richard Alpert, as a case in point. Or consider how different you feel before and after a deep meditation, a good workout, a massage, dancing, inspiring music, sexual union, or a gut wrenching belly laugh: Our vibration and attitude modulates our world. Like a caterpillar in chrysalis transforming into a butterfly, we can transform our individual reality. So collectively, particularly in a massive united effort, we can transmute the course of life and history in a similar metamorphosis.

LightShift 2000 was born from a recurring vision of divine instructions before it became manifest in a plan. Now the plan is evolving, growing, and creating itself out of the wonderful linkages, inspirations, and partnerships which are being engendered everyday. It amazes me that after billions of years of evolution—right at the shift of an age and the entrance into a new millennium—we have a global communication device through which we can all connect. We wish to use this tool for its ultimate purpose—for the common good of humanity. Our people need us, Mother Earth calls us to serve her desire to survive and thrive. We yearn to turn the current destructive direction around into a sustainable and renewable life. We hear the sound of the heavens silently beckoning us from within. We feel the heart of God calling those who live for the flame of love. When there are enough feathers on a wing, a bird is ready to fly. And when the wings gracefully synchronize, there is **flight**.

Let us come together...together as One...for this radiant millennial moment is ripe with Promise.

In the silence of our essence, we share the wellspring of creation. From this sacred place, we are given the rare opportunity for a grand alignment of spirit, a linkage of love, an awesome outpouring of hope. You, my friend, are the LightShift...the hope of the future.

January 1, 2000 is the radiant millennial moment when we can assemble as this quantum of humanity necessary to form this awesome core of light. You are invited, welcomed, and blessed to be part of this core. Let us join together in unity from our vast diversity, where the divinity in all of us radiantly glows. For together...

We Will Turn On The Light of the World!

"A joyful heart is the inevitable result of a heart
burning with love"
—Mother Theresa

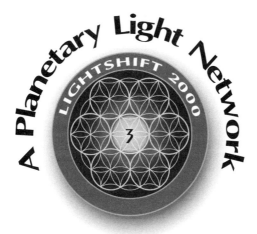

Right at the shift of the ages and the turn of the millennium—just as civilization finds itself at a critical crossroads—a global information system has emerged capable of instantaneously connecting all of us. Simultaneously, humanity finds itself in a rapid spiritual awakening—what has been described as an acceleration, a grand catharsis, a quickening, a christing of consciousness. The Earth has grown a brain, expanded its mind, and is discovering its destiny in a planetary network of light. The combination illuminates the lamp of **HOPE.**

For thirty years, a French Jesuit Priest named Teilhard de Chardin wrote a variety of works which inspired James Lovelock's **Gaia Hypothesis:** The global ecosystem as a living superorganism, whose whole is far greater than the sum of its parts. He envisioned a stage of evolution where a complex membrane of information fueled by human consciousness enveloped our planet crystallizing into "a noosphere" (from the Greek noo, for mind). This global nervous system membrane is biological, spiritual, and technological; increasing neurons and expanding spiritual awareness in humans combined with advancing electronics in technology has given birth to a planetary thought network; a global net of self-awareness, instantaneous feedback, and planetary communication. As Chardin portrays this process, **"a glow ripples outward from the first spark** of conscious reflection; the point of ignition grows larger and the fire spreads in ever-widening circles, until finally the whole planet is covered with incandescence." Humankind is heading for an **"Omega Point,"** an exciting convergence where the spiritual and technological fusion of Earth and human are birthing a vibrant consciousness leading to a new state of peace, passion, and planetary unity.

Though pre-internet, Chardin was certainly envisioning cyberspace as the technological component of the membrane: A vast electronic nervous system encircling the Earth through a constellation of connections of phone lines, satellites, and computer circuits coalescing into "the living unity of a single tissue," of collective thoughts. Or as John Perry Barlow summarized, **"The point of all evolution up to this stage is the creation of a collective organism of Mind."** But Chardin fervently and astutely insisted, "it is not just our heads or our bodies which we must bring together, but our hearts...humanity is building its composite brain beneath our eyes...its **Heart**—without which the ultimate wholeness of its power of unification can never be achieved."

We are now evolving a new awareness of the Earth as a conscious entity unified with its human residents, synchronistically and synergistically awakening. We are transitioning from experiencing the Earth as a physical biosphere, to knowing it as a noosphere—a miraculous organism with a mind and a heart, as well as a body. In this stage in the evolution of consciousness, an awakened humanity is merging through its spiritual and technological interconnectedness as Earth's new organ of spontaneous consciousness.

As a vital part of our alive and conscious Earth, at the very essence of our humanity, we acknowledge the Great Spirit of unity and love at the heart of virtually all spiritual traditions. So beyond any diverse dogmas or varying beliefs, what we all share when we put our ideas aside and join together in meditation or prayer is this same Great Spirit radiating at the source of our existence from the core of our hearts. Here we merge as One in heart, mind, and spirit, as the vital and transformative consciousness of the whole.

THE INNERNET: THOUGHTS HAVE WINGS

Just as seven oceans connect all the land masses of Earth, or the sky links all regions of our planet, we are also connected through the medium of thought waves. On the inner plane, we are all subtly connected energetically on the **"innernet."** Because this energy is invisible, many people do not understand or accept this concept. Others, including myself, know how powerful our internal reality is in creating our external circumstances. Though operating on a more subtle level, thought waves are transmitted by the same scientific principles underlying the transmission of sound or light which powers telephones, the internet, radios, televisions, satellites, and other high technologies. Thought is vibration. At the source, all beings emanate from the highest and clearest source of light in the universe, referred to by most people as God or Spirit. In silence and clarity, here we may all unite in a planetary network of light.

The LightShift 2000 project is merging these two naturally evolving spiritual and technological forces for a noble higher purpose: to elevate the unified field of collective consciousness of humanity. Using the internet and other advanced and conventional technologies to organize, synchronize, and unify the unlimited beauty, passion, and power of the human spirit, we intend to bring together a critical mass of humanity on the "innernet," to help create the mindset for a turnaround in the course of human civilization.

Like the interconnected circles of the LightShift logo, one key will be for the entire global family to discard little differences and join hands in the beautiful spirit of universal love. We must now live larger than before. Many divisive and dogmatic walls blocking the natural flow of spirit must come tumbling down.

Another key will be for the various inspired individuals and groups who are working on transformational projects for a renewable, sustainable, and brighter future to find connecting points to amalgamate and focalize their inspired energy into unified endeavors. We have the need, the tools, the resources, the power, and the passion.

Now, we must bring this all into alignment with universal love and enlightened vision.

The challenge of the new millennium will be for us to come together and open up our miraculous hearts, embrace the unity of the human family, and respond boldly to the true needs of the collectivity with beauty and inspiration.

Bright new hope illuminates tomorrow. In **Earth in the Balance**, Al Gore inspired by Chardin wrote, **"armed with such faith we might find it possible to resanctify the Earth, identify her as God's creation, and accept our responsibility to protect and defend her."**

And, for the very first time in the span of human history, the entire human family is joining hearts in a series of shining moments of collective attunement, changing forever the inner sense and view we have with others—no longer disconnected and diverse strangers from distant traditions or faraway lands—but true brothers and sisters with a common purpose in a universal Circle of Life: A Planetary Light Network.

"Someday, after we have mastered the winds, the waves, the tides and gravity, we shall harness for God the energies of love. Then, for the second time in the history of the world, we will have discovered fire."

—Pierre Teilhard de Chardin (1881-1955)

The Blessing

This brilliant Spirit
the essence we all share
bursting seeds of new consciousness
this life we all dare

From the molten magma of pure life force
a vibrant rainbow flame has now awakened
opening our hearts and minds
to ever brighter dimensions of love and light

We are the Ignition....
spiraling Starbursts in a Supernova
of Radiance
Perpetually interlinked
by the incandescent chord of holy Spirit
we breathe this smile of God and
feel the eternal OM of the Heavens.........Ommmmmm

So let us soar Beyond....
Blazing brilliant trails into the unknown
Exploring our vast luminosity
Beyond mind....beyond form

Into incandescent sparkles of glowing divinity
dancing in rapture and surrender
with Mother Earth through the cycles of life
weaving the sacred tapestry
of infinite heart and soul....

We are a magic rainbow......
a synergistic unity
riding upon the crest
of the wave of destiny.

WE ARE....
All the love in the Universe

WE ARE....We Will....and We Can....be God's Will

MAY we serve this light from within
and spread our golden sunshine
throughout this sacred Land, forever
into Eternity

D oes the quality of our consciousness affect our lives? Absolutely! Think how differently you feel before and after a vigorous workout, a good laugh, a massage, an uplifting movie, a walk in nature, a symphony or concert, or a peaceful meditation. Or, consider the difference in vibrational energy between experiencing a punk rock concert or a meditation ashram. Since we are all energetically connected, when our own individual states of mind and lives are changed, wouldn't this influence the energy of the community, the society, and thus, the course of events? The positive affect of meditation on both personal and planetary transformation is no longer a matter of speculation, but a **proven scientific certainty**.

THE MAHARISHI EFFECT

All forms of meditation are pathways to the great source of love and light at the center of our being, as are many other ways. Like the epithet, "one light, many paths," there are lots of doorways to the divine, and many effective meditation methods. Though it would be difficult to determine which is the best form of meditation, the Maharishi Mahesh Yogi's Transcendental Meditation technique (TM) certainly has collected the most scientific documentation for its efficacy. While this vast body of research was specifically done for this particular method, many people feel these benefits would apply to all forms of meditation.

David Orme-Johnson, Ph.D., Dean of Research of the Maharishi University of Management has compiled and edited a vast and powerful archive of scientific research on the benefits of the TM technique—the most significant body of evidence in the world on any program for developing human potential. Over 500 scientific studies from 200 independent universities and institutions in 33 countries have been published in over 100 leading scientific journals. Their conclusions all scientifically verify that meditation benefits virtually every area of life.

This global research documents TM's effectiveness for all cultural and ethnic groups, all socioeconomic levels, and all intellectual ranges. Furthermore, every age group benefits—from increased alertness in infants of meditating parents—to increased health, happiness, and longevity in the meditating elderly.

Scores of studies have also found that the reduction of stress in meditators creates a powerful influence of harmony in the energy of the environment at large. Scientists have named this phenomenon the **Maharishi Effect**—the finding that when just 1% of the population is meditating, the overall quality of life improves for everyone. This has been demonstrated, scientifically measured, and documented by a reduction in the symptoms of social stress such as delinquency, traffic accidents, and illness, as well as a reduction in political conflicts and improvement in international relations. **Mass synchronized meditation** has been proven to be the most powerful and effective technology for the implementation of World Peace!

M E D I T A T I O N A N D W O R L D P E A C E

Maharishi asserts that the single and most potent ecological influence is a pervasive unified field of collective consciousness—the collective influence of the consciousness of individuals that embody a society. Stressed individuals create an atmosphere of distress in the collective consciousness, influencing the thinking and actions of everyone. This is the same unified field Einstein and quantum physics recently discovered. Maharishi maintains that criminal behavior, drug abuse, armed conflict, and the other features of social stress are more than just the problem of individuals. Rather, the root cause is distress in the unified field of collective consciousness.

Maharishi concludes that the only practical way to heal large-scale problems is to approach them holistically—by creating coherence in the collective consciousness. Citing the general principle of science, that the coherent elements of a system exert an influence proportional to their number squared, Maharishi has estimated that 1% of the population practicing meditation would be enough to create an influence of coherence in collective consciousness capable of neutralizing the stresses which are the root cause of social problems.

Since 1979, published research has concluded that when a group of meditators located anywhere in the world is sufficiently large, that is, approaching the square root of 1% of the world population (7700), international relations improve and regional conflicts decrease world-wide! There are fewer violent deaths due to homicides, suicides, and traffic fatalities, a reduction in unemployment and inflation; and a general improvement in the overall quality of life.

This vast body of research concludes that the only viable means of reducing and eventually eliminating the age-old problems of society and creating world peace is the **systemic** approach of creating coherence and enlivening the unified field of collective consciousness. This is precisely the intention and purpose of the LightShift 2000 project: To create a quantum World Peace system of which we can all be a vital part.

The Maharishi research also documents the enormous physical and mental benefits of meditation.

P H Y S I C A L   B E N E F I T S

Large health insurance studies have found that TM meditators in all age groups display a 50% reduction in both inpatient and out-patient medical care. Hospitalization is 87% lower for heart disease and 55% lower for cancer! Even more remarkable, meditators over 40 years old have approximately 70% fewer medical problems than others in their age group, and individuals in their mid-50s have a biological age twelve years younger than their chronological age!

M E N T A L   B E N E F I T S

Numerous studies have found that the practice of TM increases comprehension and improves the ability to focus, and is the best means of reducing anxiety, depression, and anger. Transcendental consciousness, the experience of one's higher Self, becomes a stable internal frame of reference, providing an unshakable sense of self. Meditators tend to perceive the world more positively and holisti-cally. Creativity increases, as measured by tests of both verbal and pictorial fluency, flexibility, and originality. Perception becomes more accurate and less driven by preconceptions and misconcep-tions. Basic memory processes improve. School children who prac-tice TM significantly improve in mathematics, reading, language and study skills within a semester. Studies of elementary school stu-dents, high school students, college students, and adults have found markedly increased IQ scores compared to non-meditators.

As Dr. Orme Johnson summarizes, "meditation is unparalleled in its ability to develop the unique and full potential of the individual, making a person more self-sufficient, spontaneous, productive, more capable of meeting challenges, and developing warm interpersonal relationships."

Taking daily dips into the sacred silent space within accesses a trea-sure chest of internal dimensions, and an eternal fountain of regen-eration from the source of creation.

CRITICAL MASS

There are far more radical claims for the power of meditation. Accounts of Tibetan lamas melting snow to stay warm in the Himalayas, levitation, spoon bending, and other paranormal feats are becoming common. The ability of the focused mind is awesome. In any event, four primary benefits have been established:

* Meditation focuses and improves the quality of consciousness.
* Focused consciousness improves the quality of our own lives.
* Meditation and mass meditation increases the resonance of the unified field of collective consciousness.
* A more harmonious unified field reduces social stress and positively enhances the overall quality of life. The family that prays together, stays together.

The concept of critical mass was popularized by a social science study known as the **Hundredth Monkey Phenomena,** authored by author Ken Keyes Jr., which I share with you in case you are not familiar with it.

THE HUNDREDTH MONKEY
A STORY ABOUT SOCIAL CHANGE.

The Japanese monkey, Macaca fuscata, had been observed in the wild for a period of over 30 years. In 1952, on the island of Koshima, scientists were providing monkeys with sweet potatoes dropped in the sand. The monkey liked the taste of the raw sweet potatoes, but they found the dirt unpleasant. An 18-month-old female named Imo found she could solve the problem by washing the potatoes in a nearby stream. She taught this trick to her mother. Her playmates also learned this new way and they taught their mothers too.

This cultural innovation was gradually picked up by various monkeys before the eyes of the scientists. Between 1952 and 1958 all the young monkeys learned to wash the sandy sweet potatoes to make them more palatable. Only the adults who imitated their children learned this social improvement. Other adults kept eating the dirty sweet potatoes.

Then something startling took place. In the autumn of 1958, a certain number of Koshima monkeys were washing sweet potatoes— the exact number is not known. Let us suppose that when the sun rose one morning there were 99 monkeys on Koshima Island who had learned to wash their sweet potatoes. Let's further suppose that later that morning, *the hundredth monkey* learned to wash potatoes.

THEN IT HAPPENED! By that evening almost everyone in the tribe was washing sweet potatoes before eating them. The added energy of this hundredth monkey somehow created an ideological breakthrough!

But notice: A most surprising thing observed by these scientists was that the habit of washing sweet potatoes then jumped over the sea. Colonies of monkeys on other islands and the mainland troop of monkeys at Takasakiyama began washing their sweet potatoes. Thus, when a certain critical number achieves an awareness, this new awareness may be communicated from mind to mind. Although the exact number may vary, this **Hundredth Monkey Phenomenon** means that when only a limited number of people know of a new way, it may remain the conscious property of these people.

But there is a point at which if only one more person tunes in to a new awareness, a field is strengthened so that this awareness is picked up by **almost everyone!**

THE MAGIC NUMBER

There is great debate as to just what the magic quantity of human catalysts constitute the quantum number to reach a critical mass which will trigger an explosion in global consciousness, capable of transforming all of humanity. There are various wavelengths on this issue. The most popular is that critical mass is one tenth of one percent of the world's population of 6 billion, or 6 million. Another school feels it will take one percent, or 60 million. The Maharishi formula calculates the magic number based on a scientific principle as the square root of the world population, or 7700. Osho Rajneesh said, "if we can create 10,000 buddhas, that is enough to save humanity." One thing is for certain: More is better. So we invite you to join the LightShift: For you may just be the **"hundredth human."**

THE UNIFIED FIELD

PRINCESS DIANA AND THE UNIFIED FIELD

A significant portion of human consciousness was unified in mourning for beloved Princess Diana, "a shining light on Earth, a brilliant star in heaven." It was a magnificent outpouring of the full spectrum of human emotion; a mixture of all the forms of love from pomp, to passion, to profound sadness.

Yet it is unfortunate that it takes tragedy to bring the human family together. Wouldn't it be wonderful to come together with foresight and grand intention in radiant love rather than sorrow: To act rather than react, to celebrate rather than mourn. As Mohatma Ghandhi once said, **"prayer from the heart can achieve what nothing else can in this world."** A unified field of consciousness, possibly a critical mass was gathered during the Princess Diana funeral. Yet it was a reaction to catastrophe which pulled the human community together in sadness (as was the case with JFK, RFK, MLK, John Lennon, etc. etc.). Our LightShift hope and wish is to reverse this trend: Let's gather the human family together in brilliant spirit with grand intention—for together, we can cocreate miracles. I think Princess Diana and Mother Theresa are smiling on us, blessing and assisting us in orchestrating this millennial miracle from above.

THE ROLLING STONES, SANTANA AND OPRAH

I am humbled and honored to be a part of the LightShift series of meditations, and can attest to the exhilaration I feel everyday and every month at Noon during these shining times of collective attunement. And as this effulgent wave of light builds everyday toward critical mass, I look most forward to being a radiant cell in the luminous body of humanity which will merge in pure light in quantum numbers for the New Year's Eve meditations to ignite the spiritual light of the world.

Yet, there are also numerous musical events already gathering huge numbers of people that also unify consciousness through the medium of sound and spirit, that could further boost the unified field with resonance to a higher octave. Imagine, if at a Rolling Stones concert for example, Mick Jagger led a few minutes of silent or sound meditation with a capacity crowd at Dodger stadium! Outlandish? I'd like to put this forth as a challenge to all those who have the power and care about the future of humankind. I hope a group like Santana will catch this wonderful wave of spirit. And what if the new thought television networks like **Oasis** or **Millennium** programmed times for collective attunements, hopefully aligned with the LightShift events. Or how about the wonderful and charismatic Oprah Winfrey getting into the act? Mass meditation and prayer has been proven to work wonders. We invite everyone to come together in the pure spirit of love to help boost the unified field. The time has come for all of us to be a radiant spark of the LightShift.

"Come on people now, Smile on your Brother, Everybody get
Together; Try and Love one another right Now."
—The Youngbloods

I know that when I think, feel, speak and act in unity, my life flows like a river to the sea. These simple alignments within myself engage the process of spontaneous manifestation, otherwise known as a miracle. I know that the supreme intelligence, the divine mind that manifested the miracle of creation is a unified force field of pure light energy. I know this unified field through my heart as love. I know my spirit is brilliant light, encased in a body of matter. I also know that in any moment, I can align with this creative intelligence and find peace, abundance, and joy, for God loves us so prolificly. And I know that only in alignment can there be fulfillment and manifestation.

The bible says, "with God all things are possible." Spirit indeed knows no limits. I know that when I surrender my heart in deep love and devotion to God, I align with my soul, my spirit, my gifts and talents, my purpose, and my will. Here I am in the creative vortex of the wave of life where everything flows, grows, and glows in the light of the miracle of creation.

Congestion of the life force on any level is the cause of illness or disease; clarity the source of health and power. If we are confused in our mind, we cannot act; when we are emotionally upset we feel down or depressed, and when we have a physical ailment, our bodies feel pain which influences how we think and feel. Removing the blockages to the flow of spirit through our bodies, our hearts, and our minds is the universal solvent which brings us back into alignment and peace.

For every single particle of our physical body, every fiber of our being is in communion with each particle in the cosmos. Every space within our physical body communicates with all spaces in the universe. Energy and matter flow without interruption between the universe and us. Our thoughts extend to and from universal thought—our mind flows seamlessly within the cosmic mind sea. When we know, feel and unify with this spiritual presence, we are the **presence**. When we allow God's energy to dance through our being, we are in alignment with our spiritual center—our primary alignment.

Light is the eternal spark—the metabolic flame that vitalizes the body. When we are in our spiritual center, it radiates pure light, and the mind and heart and soul are all consecrated in union with the divine current—here we are truly alive and aligned in the energy of the sacred. This is the powerful, irresistible and natural healing current of the divine force. This is the direction we are evolving, and where we wish to elevate the world. There is a synchronous acceleration in the lightbodies of Gaia. By connecting in the fusion process of meditation and prayer with quantum numbers of other human beings in this radiant spirit, miracles are born and generated. For here, congestion, disease, discomfort, and darkness, are spun off and released as this whirling power courses through the primary alignment—the "cosmic consciousness," the kundalini, that sacred chord of energy that connects all souls to God and pure being through love. It is in our silence where we contact and merge with the light of Spirit.

The very best and source of us is love. That is the simple truth of our being, that deep inside, past our pain, we are all God's love. It's simply a matter of opening up to our love inside. And when we do this, something wonderful happens in the world, which is a miracle.

Close your eyes and let your mind expand
Let no fear of death or darkness arrest its course
Allow your mind to merge with Mind
Let it flow out upon the great curve of consciousness
Let it soar on the wings of the great bird of duration
Up to the very Circle of Eternity
—HERMES

God, the ultimate source of energy and divine love, radiates as light equally through all hearts of every being, no matter what religion, lack of religion, race, belief, nationality, or net worth. Light and love are immutable, despite what they are named or how they are perceived. There is no power greater than God, and our capacity to receive, give, and share love and light is our richest treasure. This treasure is accessed through our consciousness. When we are simply being true to our self, our alignment with Spirit ignites the magical fountain of miracles from the infinite well of light in the universe.

In the beginning there was God, the Source of Light.
He is the one Lord of all beings. He upholds
the Earth and the Heavens.
He it is to whom we offer our oblations.
—Rig Veda

THE MAGIC OF AFFIRMATION

Affirmation means "to make firm." Affirmations are positive statements which consciously focus the intention of achieving a desired positive result. They are restorative, creative, healing, strengthening, energizing, and uplifting upgrades to our internal computer, affirming that a condition already exists. They are such powerful tools for personal transformation, that they are a form of **magic**. When we affirm, we are declaring a positive statement which goes out to the world and the entire universe, which boomerangs quickly into being. Affirmations work on many levels. They are a means of transmitting from our higher self, and communicating with our own and other people's conscious and unconscious minds. The power of affirmation is limited only by our personal conviction. If we are fully centered in manifesting the affirmation, it will soon be!

Use them at the beginning of the day, in times of weakness, turmoil, or pain, to initiate a new venture, at the beginning or end of a meditation or prayer, or at bedtime. They will trigger self empowerment and insight and produce positive changes in your body, mind, emotions and spirit. They help open your access to miracle consciousness.

30 AFFIRMATIONS FOR SHIFTING LIGHT

I align my mind and heart with all the intelligence
and goodness of Spirit
to realize the true abundance intended for me

I trust my higher Self
I listen with love to my inner voice
and release all that is unlike love

I know in each moment
I am free to choose

I know my attitude completely
shapes my reality

I know any time I spend in anger
Is time lost not being happy

I know I am fully responsible for everything
that happens in my life

My past is nothing more than the path I've left behind
What drives my life now is the energy I generate
in each of my present moments

By forgiving, I release my past

Reflecting on the path of my past unlocks a treasure chest
to learn from and do better than

I release my doubts by knowing
there is a valid reason for everything that happens

I know my life is a creation of my mind

I know my challenges are the gateways
to my personal growth and happiness

I know even in the moments which seem impossible
There **is** an Answer

I know that every moment of my life is infinitely creative
And the Universe is endlessly bountiful

I know if I project a clear enough request
Everything in my heart will manifest

I realize I am always free to let go and observe my life

I know that my problems are really opportunities
To create solutions which lead to my growth

I let go of my regrets about the past
and my anxieties about the future

I know my faith leads to my success
and my fear and doubt creates my failures

The closer I listen
the more profound the Silence becomes

I know that my Highest Self
is always present to elevate me

to the real world beyond my senses

I know I can connect my mind to be One
with the Divine Mind where there is peace in any moment

I know my self love grants my access to all love

I know I am invigorated as I seek to make Truth
my personal reality

I know that at the very essence of my Being
the way of transforming my Life is through Love

My judgements prevent me from seeing the good
that lies beyond appearances
I release my judgements to know what is real

I know I am already whole
I need not chase after anything to be complete

I am aware I do not need to dominate anyone
To be spiritually awake

I will live this day from my purest intentions
for the highest good of all

I will radiate my Sacred Self outward
for the collective good of all as a radiant spark of the LightShift

"Like a bird on the wing I fly toward the sun. I sing in my heart
so that all I meet may hear."
—Dwal Khul

THE CIRCLE

A circle is 360 degrees. It is not a straight line. It is not a box. It is not a pyramid. A circle radiates energy in all directions, like the Sun. Eyes, mandalas, and angel's haloes are all circular. Zero, the most essential number in mathematics is a circle. The Tibetan Mandala principle refers to the cyclic manifestations of the energy of the phenomenal world. In his theory of relativity, Einstein found that light travels in circular waves. Circles have no beginning or end. Humankind's most useful invention, the wheel, is circular. In Zen Buddhism, the circle symbolizes enlightenment and the perfection of humanity in unity with the primal principle. Circles are powerful. This is why most spiritual councils are held in circles, as well as many prayer groups. The circle is a symbol of creation, infinity, eternity, connection, perfection, and unity. It is often used as the symbol for God.

SACRED GEOMETRY AND THE FLOWER OF LIFE

The Flower of Life within the circle of the LightShift logo is a geometric pattern composed of nineteen interlocking circles inscribed in a sphere. In numerology, 1 + 9 = 10 = the number of unity. The foremost quality of the image is the interconnectedness of all energy. This pattern, which contains the Tree of Life, the Fruit of Life, and the Seed of Life has been found at different times all over the planet by cultures who had no contact—in England, Egypt, Ireland, Turkey, India, and Tibet. Most creation accounts, from the scientific "Big Bang" theory, the Great Void of Eastern tradition, to the Hebrew bible explain that Spirit, energy, or God created the universes out of nothingness. How indeed **does** formless eternal spirit create all the myriad forms of manifested creation? For billions of years, the magnetic energy of the universe has been attracting atoms, molecules, and cells into organic forms and systems. The language of light, also known as sacred geometry, explains that the energy of Spirit was projected in simple spherical patterns from the Great Void through the universe as the template from which all form, all processes, all manifestations, even consciousness came into being. The image of the Flower of Life is itself, the very generator of creation behind all language, music, life forms, physical laws, all structure, everything. Simply gazing at the image will animate your own process of creation and help activate your miracle consciousness.

Other patterns that emerge from the Flower of Life are the star-tetrahedron and six pointed Star of David. See if you can visualize them emanating from the seven main circles of the Flower. It is purported that all life forms emanate energy fields which match the geometry of the star tetrahedron. Richard Hoagland of Nasa has identified the geometry of this pattern with its 19.5 degree vectors in everything from the human body to the pyramids on Mars and Earth, and in energetic grid zones throughout the solar system, such as the gigantic Red Spot on Jupiter.

THE FLOWER OF LIFE AS A MODEL FOR EMPOWERMENT

Though the symbol has many other rich esoterics for which there are various workshops, the image itself provides a model for perfect resonance and cocreation for the empowerment of social synergy. This is the cornerstone of all transformational group endeavors, including projects for global change and world peace. As we are all light at the core, humans aligning with like-minded humans create the nucleus of all positive social organization in an invisible frequency of union and resonance in a field of love and light.

Visualize each circle in the flower as a group, and the petals within the circle as the people in the group. Each part adds its synergistic light to the field of love, raising the consciousness of the whole far beyond the individual components. Now consider the connecting points between the circles as the flashpoints of resonance where boundaries dissolve and cocreation surges as synergistic jumps in consciousness and manifestation. By connecting in radiance and love bonded by our passion to unleash the gifts and talents of each member, we can form enlightened teams around grand intentions. And by each team or circle connecting at the points of resonance with other teams, we can coalesce and synergize our energy into the enlightened process of cocreation. The Flower of Life thus provides an organizational blueprint for the evolution and generation of the spirit of creation and the manifestation of miracles.

THE FLOWER OF LIFE AS A MODEL FOR THE UNITY OF HUMANITY

Imagine each petal in the flower as an individual, each a vital cell in the radiant body of humanity. Consider each circle as one of the world's great spiritual traditions, religions, paths, or non-paths, emanating from a central point of light. The connecting points of resonance between the petals and the circles illustrate that at the core, beyond our thoughts, we are all One.

"The universe is a great temple, the stars its lights, the Earth its altar, all corporeal beings its fiery sacrificers, and man, the priest of the Eternal, offers the sacrifices."
—Louis Claude de Saint-Martin

THE ARCHETYPE OF LIGHT

The Good above all light is called a Spiritual Light because it is an originating beam. An overflowing radiance, illuminating with its fullness every mind above the world, around it or within it, renewing all spiritual powers, embracing them all by its transcendent elevation. It contains within itself in simple form, the entire ultimate principle of light as the transcendent archetype of light. And while bearing this light in its womb, it exceeds it in quality and precedes it in time, conjoining together all spiritual and rational beings, uniting them as One.
—Dionysius the Areopagite

Light, that originating force of life and spirit, is the unifying bond all beings share. In our resounding inner silence, we all connect in radiance. When we examine the numerology of the word light, we derive the formula: $12+9+7+8+20=38=11$. Eleven is a master number in numerology, and the number of the ten attributes of the Sefiroth of the Kaballah plus the Divine representing the process of cocreation of all and everything. It is also the number of the 11th astrological sign Aquarius, the sign of the age we have just entered, representing the divine marriage of our masculine and feminine nature, unity, cooperation, friendship, and synergy.

THE POWER OF SYNERGY

Visualize a pair of graceful Olympic synchronized swimmers doing their magnificent water dance. Suddenly one of the partners cramps and must leave the pool, while the other completes the routine. The magic of their synergy is lost—and eventhough half the team is still doing the same precise maneuvers; the beauty, elegance, and magnificence of their relational creation is missing.

"We" can be so much more powerful than **"me."** Each of us has different talents and abilities, which when creatively connected can create magical and expansive combinations. Consider a four member band, like **The Beatles,** composed of Ringo Starr on drums, Paul McCartney on base, George Harrison on lead guitar, and John Lennon on rhythm guitar. Imagine listening only to Ringo beating on his drums, Paul laying down his base lines, George playing his leads, and John his rhythms, individually at different times. They probably wouldn't even hold your interest for long. But together, they were a miracle.

The eminent futurist Buckminster Fuller invented the term synergy, defining it as "synthesis plus energy." Webster's Dictionary, defines synergism as "an ancient theological doctrine holding that in regeneration there is cooperation of divine grace and human activity." The ancient Greeks were also aware of the law of increase through partnership. They observed that the life force responds and magnifies through *agape*, the quality of brotherly and sisterly love. The Greek word *synergos* translates as "working together." The Law of Synergy also appears in The Bible in Matthew 18:20, when he says "For where two or three are gathered together in my name There Am I in the midst of them."

Our foremost and greatest partner is the universe itself. The simple affirmation, **"I am in synergy with the universe,"** exponentially amplifies and enhances our potency, as we are invoking all the invisible forces of nature, our spirit guides, our angels, and all other agents of spirit.

Synergy expands through cooperation and collaboration. As Euclid once said, "the whole is greater than the sum of its parts." Energy is generated in cooperative endeavors which magnifies the capabilities of individuals acting alone, in most circumstances. Spirit is multiplicative, not simply additive, and stimulates additional charges which cannot be quantified. When we align with each other creatively in love and pure intention for good, the combined energy creates a dynamic and multidimensional expansion, well beyond the simple addition of our individual efforts. Synergy is a way in which Spirit supports and rewards healthy relationships, particularly those connected by purposeful service to the greater whole.

Human energy is aligned with spirit when it manifests as love, wisdom, and grace. In synergy, humanity has the ability to effortlessly expand good, anytime an agreement is made or an intention is stated. Synergy is a natural magic of universal law, which exists in our infinitely abundant and compassionate universe. Anytime we connect in a synergistic relationship, we wield a mighty alchemical tool for healing ourselves, each other, and the Earth. Synergy is a key to the doorway of the geometric expansion of consciousness, inherently amplifying the greater good. Synergistic activity engages us as potent and conscious co-creators—active agents in our grand catharsis and awakening into the higher consciousness of unity through our harmony in diversity.

When we synergize together in meditation or prayer, we magnify and project our shared vision of wholeness through the unified field of consciousness into manifestation. This assists and empowers all endeavors in resonance with the greater good, and has simultaneous reciprocal benefits for both our personal and planetary transformation. And as we align and connect in synergistic teams, we form the very core of the process of evolution and the spirit of creation.

THE MIRACLE

FROM THE CONCEPTION THE INCREASE
FROM THE INCREASE THE SWELLING
FROM THE SWELLING THE THOUGHT
FROM THE THOUGHT THE REMEMBRANCE,
FROM THE REMEMBRANCE, THE CONSCIOUSNESS,
THE PASSION

FROM THE NOTHING THE BEGETTING
FROM THE BEGETTING THE INCREASE
FROM THE INCREASE THE ABUNDANCE
FROM THE ABUNDANCE, THE BOUNDLESS
FROM THE BOUNDLESS, THE SELF
THE LIVING BREATH,
THE MIRACLE

Connecting with God

LIGHTSHIFT 2000

6

One primary objective of LightShift 2000 is to get more of the human family meditating: The family that prays together, stays together! This achieves two wonderful things: it helps create resonance in the unified field of consciousness, and shares one of the greatest gifts for enhancing life. Stilling our restless minds is one of the finest ways to access our cosmic consciousness and supreme wisdom, which we all have inside. Stimulation rather than stillness causes our mental energy to be in perpetual motion. Meditation attunes the scattered spray of the light of our thoughts into a focused laser beam of clear and powerful consciousness. Consider meditation like a tune-up for your mind, just as you would tune a musical instrument before you play. In this elevated frequency we may drink from the divine fountain of the infinite wisdom and peace of our higher Self. Here we may experience ultimate reality while living on this Earth.

Just as there is one ocean with many waves, there are many methods of meditation. I offer you the following basic technique.

A S I M P L E   U N I V E R S A L   M E D I T A T I O N

* **The Setting:** Sit or lay down in a safe, comfortable, quiet place, where you can let go of any tension or cares.

* **Intention:** Set an intention to let go of everything and embrace your inner peace, joy, and love.

* **Attention:** Close your eyes, relax completely, and focus only on your breath, which should be full and rhythmic.

* **Release:** Release any thoughts, sensations, or emotions and let them pass like clouds in the sky until they disappear and your inner sky is clear. If they reappear, release them with each exhale. Tap into the blissful Silent Space within you.

* **Imagine:** Imagine your entire being filling up with light from the pure essence within you.

* **Focus:** Focus on a point such as your third eye. Imagine your inner light expanding outward, radiating through and beyond your aura, out in all directions expanding through the entire universe. Let everything else disappear.

* **Sound:** You may wish to optionally use a mantra such as **AAAHH** or **OM** silently or in a resonant tone with each exhale.

* **Absorption:** Feel your unity with the One Great Mind and Heart of Spirit. During the global meditations, allow yourself to feel and embrace the radiance of all the beautiful spirits who are also meditating, and absorb all the love, light, peace, and joy in the universe.

Meditation is the crown jewel of most systems of yoga from the East. Being the highest of the yogas, it is also the simplest, purest, and clearest. The essence of meditation is to stop the mind from becoming lost in random thoughts, and instead focused in pure consciousness. This mind exercise is helpful for grasping new knowledge and information, for tapping into our intuitive under-standing beyond language, and for obtaining a fresh, uncluttered glimpse of our own lives and being in the universe. The gift of med-itation is inner peace and spiritual wisdom.

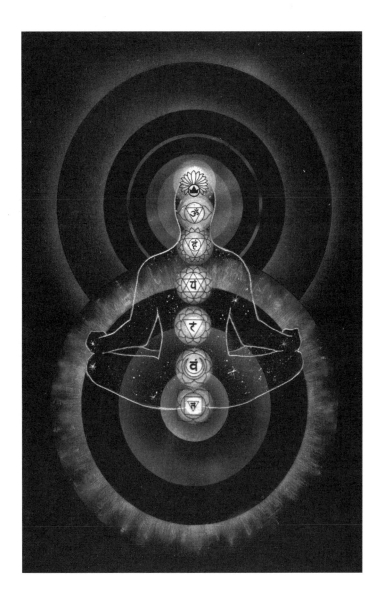

The goal of meditation is to experience directly, without any kind of perceptually conditioned filters. The meditation experience is thus, the same as the nature of reality itself. When we practice meditation regularly, we realize that the natural and aware state of mind is always present. Only our mental concepts stand in the way of experiencing this state of pure consciousness.

Mind has three basic qualities—clarity, luminosity, and boundlessness, which resonate from three areas of being: Clarity from the realm of mind, luminosity from the plane of spirit, and boundlessness from the dimension of will. Meditation unifies these qualities in the singularity of the moment.

"if there is no meditation, then you are like a blind man in a world of great beauty, light, and colour."

—J Krisnamurti

SOME FAVORITE PRAYERS

But if in prayer a person joins
His whole self in every word,
All the secret meanings
Enter the word of their own accord
Every letter becomes a complete World.
What a great thing he does!
Worlds above are awakened by his prayer
Thus should your prayer be Fire...
For every letter awakens worlds above

—Za wa 'at Rivash

Dear Lord,
make me an instrument of thy peace,
where there is hatred, let me sow love
where there is injury, pardon,
where there is doubt, faith,
where there is despair, hope,
where there is darkness, light,
where there is sadness, joy

O, Divine Master
grant that I may not so much seek
to be consoled as to console,
to be understood as to understand,
to be loved as to love
For it is in giving that we receive,
it is in pardoning that we are pardoned
and it is in dying that we are born
to eternal life.

—St Francis of Assisi

The Declaration of Divinity
Ware Soku Kami Nari
I am a Divine Being

The words I speak are the words of God.
The Thoughts I emit are the thoughts of God.
The actions I take are the actions of God.

The words, thoughts, and actions of God
are abundantly overflowing
with infinite love, infinite wisdom, infinite joy,
infinite energy, infinite power, infinite success and infinite supply.
They are nothing more, nothing less.
Therefore (Ware Soku Kami Nari)
I am a Divine Being
Who speaks, thinks, and acts just as God does.
I will brighten and elevate myself

To become none other than God
So that when others see me they cannot help
But think they have seen God.

Those who have seen me have seen God.
I emanate light and continue to radiate
the most supreme infinite love of God
to all humanity.

THE GREAT INVOCATION
(Original Version)

From the point of Light within the Mind of God,
Let Light stream forth into the minds of Men.
Let Light descend on Earth.

From the Point of Love within the Heart of God
Let love stream forth into the hearts of men.
May Christ return to Earth.

From the center where the Will of God is known
Let purpose guide the little wills of men
The purpose which the Masters know and serve.

From the center which we call the race of men
Let the Plan of Love and Light work out
And may it seal the door where evil dwells.
Let Light and Love and Power restore the Plan on Earth.

THE GREAT INVOCATION for the TRUE AGE of CONSCIOUSNESS
adapted by KEN KALB
(makes a great song using C, G, F, and Am on the guitar)

From the point of Light within the Mind of God
May light illuminate our lives
May light radiate on Earth
And Empower our rebirth

From the point of Love within the Heart of God
May love stream forth into our Hearts
May we Be the Spirit of Love

From the center which is the Will of God
May purpose guide our will
The purpose which the masters know and serve
The life of love we all deserve

From the core of love which forms the race of Human
Let the Plan of Love and Light work out
And seal the door where evil dwells
So we can turn on the Light of the World!

May Light and Love Empower the Divine plan on Earth
May Light and Love Empower our Rebirth

Sacred Circle
(Great for group prayer)

May we release all thoughts of past and future
and center in the radiance of the Eternal Now.
May we engage that eternal light connection which binds us to
each other and unify as One.
May this energy flow through us and connect
with the heart of the Great Spirit
manifest as the original vibration of OM,
the essence of All That Is.

May we feel all the blessings of this divine light flowing
through us, spiraling through each chakra,
blessing, sanctifying, and renewing us, until that energy
flows radiantly through the root chakra to
the heart of the Mother.
Here may we be cradled in dynamic balance between the
Mother and the Father, as a beloved Child of the Universe,
a vibrant and sacred part of the whole.

May we feel all the vital energy of the Universe
coursing through us as One.
For this healing, blessing, and awareness,
we give thanks.

We are all fully present in this moment,
balanced and sanctified, fully conscious at all levels,
integrated and whole. We are centered in our
Higher Self, and here we begin our work....
We come together to Will the conscious
awakening of all of humankind; an awakening to the
Higher Self—an awakening to our Oneness.

May our will be guided by the Will of God
Let us be a clear and perfect channel for
the Divine Will of the Universe,
Mother—Father God, All That Is.
May we fully be
the Light Bearers that we are.

May each human heart feel connected
To the Divine Heart of humanity
May each mind know its connection
To the Divine Mind of humanity,
May each soul express itself fully and reign gloriously
over it's vehicles of mind and personality.

May all of humanity live from the glory of the Higher Self,
May those who slumber in illusion
awaken to the Divine Reality.
May those who resist the Call to Awaken
enter the process of Self-realization.
May those who hold fast to duality
Be blessed with awakening to the Greater Reality of Oneness.
May it begin with us
For we are each radiant cells in the body of humanity
Glowing in the light of divinity
Eternally.

The Radiant Self

More radiant than the Sun
Purer than the Snows
Finer than the Ethers
Is the Self
The Spirit Within Me
I am that Self
That Self am I

"Prayer from the heart can achieve
what nothing else can in this world."
—**Mohatma Ghandi**

Since the millennium is based on a Gregorian calendar date, let's dig into the evolution of daykeeping, examine its holistic influence on our lives, and look into the future for ways to improve our method of making time in the new millennium.

Every single day of our lives we are attuned to the calendar. Day after day—each month, every year, our lives are intimately connected to dates in the temporal dimension. The calendar is truly our fundamental astronomical and astrological tool. Certain dates like birthdays and anniversaries, solstices and equinoxes, and particular calendrical synchronicities carve special cyclical significance within human consciousness. The cycle of comets Hyukatake and Hale-Bopp passing Earth precisely one year apart—memorializing ancient prophecy by demarcating the shift of the ages—is a case in point. The common factor linking spirit, psyche, and matter is *time.* Even though our calendrical system is flawed, the repeating cycles of time create deep psychological archetypes within our consciousness. Though many people are in calendar-denial, we are all very much attuned to our **"inner calendar."**

The most powerful point in any cycle is its birthing point. The initiatory thrust of a new beginning is always charged with hope and promise. Just like the birth of a romance or a child, the birth of a New Year, a new decade, or a new century are all archetypally epochal. A new millennium carries a special charge incomparable to any other date. It is not only like a thousand New Year's Eves, but much more, because it signifies a mythical and mystical threshold. ***The beginning of a new millennium is a collective psychological pregnancy potently charged by a massive floodtide of anticipation, expectation, excitement, awe, hope and wonder for the future and destiny of humankind.***

Imagine, you and a friend are boarding a spacecraft traversing the vast distances of space to land as the first beings on the Earth 60 million years ago. When the time arrived when you needed to separate to scout the land, get food, or do anything independently, you would need to create a system to synchronize and coordinate your activities. As the days passed, the Sun rose and set, the Moon waxed and waned, and the stars in the heavens rotated, you began to understand and record the rhythms and cycles of the cosmos and their relationship to Earth. When the Moon grew to full, shrank, reappeared as new, and grew again to full, you could calculate how many risings of the Sun (days) it took to complete the phases of the lunar cycle. After 13 of these **synodic** cycles, when the Sun finally returned to the precise position it occupied at your first observation, you could calculate a year. From this perspective, one can begin to appreciate the immensity, complexity, and necessity of the task of creating a calendar from scratch.

THE EVOLUTION OF ANCIENT CALENDARS

At the dawn of Western Civilization, the Sumerians devised an advanced solar calendar with 365 days. The ancient Babylonians constructed a lunisolar calendar with 12 lunar months of 30 days each, adding extra months when needed to keep in harmony with the seasons. About 6000 years ago, the ancient Egyptians replaced the lunar calendar with a 365-day solar calendar consisting of 12 months of 30 days each, with 5 days of celebration at the end. Starting on July 27, these 5 days of celebration honored the births of Osirus, Horus, Seth, Isis, and Nephthys. The New Year began on August 1, when the star Sirius rose at the same place as the Sun. This calendar was unchanged until 238 BC, when King Ptolemy III ordered an extra day be added to every fourth year, similar to the modern leap year.

THE EARLY ROMAN CALENDAR

The original Roman calendar, the root of our current system, was quite simply, a **mess**. Introduced in the 7th century BC, it had 10 months with 304 days in a year beginning with March. Later in the century, January and February were added to precede March, but because months were 29 or 30 days long, an extra one had to be added every two or three years. The days of the month were designated by the awkward method of counting backwards from three dates: the **calends**, or first of the month; the **ides**, or middle of the month, and the **nones**, or 9th day before the ides. If this weren't confusing enough, the situation degenerated to hopelessly chaotic when various Roman officials manipulated the calendar for their own purposes, such as hastening or delaying elections, prolonging their terms of office, or taking holidays.

In 45 BC, Julius Caesar commissioned the amazing astronomer Sosigenes to develop a uniform solar calendar so the entire Roman Empire could synchronize on the same system. What Sosigenes engineered was so accurately calibrated that each one-year cycle was only 11 minutes out of sync with the Earth's atomically calcu-lated (365 days, 5 hours, 48 minutes, and 45.5 seconds) transit of the Sun. This calendar, known as the **Julian** calendar, fixed the nor-mal year at 365 days, with a leap year every fourth year of 366 days. The Julian calendar also established the order of the months and the days of the week as they exist today. In 44 BC, Julius Caesar changed the name of the month Quintilis to Julius (July), after himself. Not to be outdone, his successor Augustus Caesar, renamed the sixth month Sextilis to Augustus (August) also in honor of himself, snipping a day off of February and sticking it on August to be equal to July. Augustus' modification established the length of the months still in use today.

THE NEW STYLE GREGORIAN CALENDAR

Though the Julian calendar bore no relationship to lunar cycles, it was a very accurate solar construction, with a growing flaw: The Julian year was 11 minutes (and 14 seconds) longer than the solar year. This disparity grew until 1582, when the vernal equinox fell 11 days early and church holidays, like Easter, were no longer syn-chronizing with their appropriate seasons. To adjust the vernal equinox back to March 21st—as it was initially set at the First Council of Nicaea in 325 AD—Pope Gregory XIII issued a decree dropping 11 days from the calendar as of October 4, 1582: Henceforth, October 15. To prevent any further displacement, the new Gregorian calendar, also provided that century years divisible evenly by 400 be made leap years, and all other century years be made common years. Thus, 1600 would be a leap year, while 1700, 1800, and 1900 were to be common years. 2000 will certainly be a **leap** year.

THE MILLENNIUM QUIRK

Just when does the third millennium really begin—2000 or 2001? Hotel rooms are already booked in Tonga and the other islands just west of the International Date Line for December 31, 1999, by tourists wishing to be the first to greet the new millennium, even if it is the peak of hurricane season. Yet most official institutions, including international law say they'll be arriving a year early. There seems to be a minor civil war brewing over whether January 1, 2000 or January 1, 2001 is indeed the dawning of the new millennium. Let's illuminate this issue.

THE OFFICIAL ANSWER
JANUARY 1, 2001

This date is officially endorsed by the The Royal Greenwich Observatory, the Encyclopedia Britannica, The US Naval Observatory, Webster's New Third International Dictionary, the World Almanac, and other arbirters of officialdom. The roots of this logic defying quirk trace back to a Scythian monk by the name of Dionysius Exiguus, alias Dennis the Diminutive, assigned the task of establishing a fixed date for Easter Sunday in what was to become the year 526 AD. Dennis, a sixth century abbott of a Roman monastery, worked exhaustively in Roman numerals to calculate a solid basis for the Christian church, replacing the old numbering system, **Anno Diocletiani**, where numbers were counted from the beginning of the reign of the Roman Emperor Diocletian. Using what he thought was the year of the birth of Jesus Christ as the reference point, he declared **Anno Domini**, or "Year of our Lord," as 1 AD rather than 0 AD, there being no zero in Roman numerals. As Jesus was most likely born in 4 BC, Dennis made two blunders while repairing the calendar for Easter. Henceforth, the modern calendar started with a one, which has perpetuated the "quirk" of all official decade, century, and millennium designations always being one year ahead—1001, 1501, and yes, the official millennium—2001.

BY POPULAR DEMAND:
JANUARY 1, 2000

Regardless of calendrical technicalities, people around the world will be heralding the new millennium when the 000's roll over odometrically on January 1, 2000. The year 2000 will be a landmark milestone for all humanity, as this most anticipated day promises to be a turning point in the direction of civilization. Numerous celebrations and events are planned, and hundreds of transformational projects will initiate this day of century's end and bimillennial beginning.

THE LIGHTSHIFT 2000 ANSWER: BOTH!

Oftentimes, the technical and official is not the practical or popular. January 1, 2000 may not be the official bimillennial date, but it might as well be. For a thousand years, people have been writing three digits after a one, until January 1, 2000, the most powerful date in human history. The LightShift monthly meditation program has a running start in bridging the unofficial and official millennium in radiance from the pure light within us all.

BACK TO THE FUTURE

Though Pope Gregory got Western Civilization's daytimers back on track with his Gregorian or New Style calendar, it took until the 18th century for it to be accepted throughout Europe, and until the 20th century to be used throughout the world. Great Britain didn't adopt it until 1752, and Napoleon established the Gregorian Calendar in France in 1806. Russia stubbornly stuck to the Julian system until the 1917 October Revolution, and Greece held out until 1923. Today it is the predominant calendar on the planet, with most of Earth's 6 billion residents using it as their primary synchronization device.

CONSPIRACY OR STUPIDITY?

So at the dawn of the third millennium, the dominant conceptual scheme for civil time-keeping is still the Gregorian Calendar: A 16th-century modification of a flat-Earth era device from 1 BC known as the Julian Calendar, designed as a quantum cleanup of Papal pandemonium.

The Gregorian calendar is based on 12 months of unequal length, with the dates and days of the week varying arbitrarily, with no consistency through time. Except for the solar cycle, it bears no relationship with any naturally occurring cycle. Time-keeping and scheduling, laws, financial markets and transactions in our present, post-industrial, information-age society, all rely on this anachronistic patchwork scheme whose roots are planted in the interests of men in a pre-scientific, theocratic society, with a feudal economy. What we now need is a universalized system, attuned to our expanding consciousness and rising emergence as an interconnected global culture.

Some people feel it has been intentionally configured to remove our connection with nature and the universe. It appears to me, however, to be more the evolution of bad planning, egotistical manipulation, and duct tape-style repair. Yet it takes a licking and keeps on ticking as the present clock of our Earth time jungle.

The new millennium presents a golden opportunity for a better way of keeping time. I suggest the United Nations prioritize the creation a **Global Calendar Council** to give full consideration to reform proposals, to be decided by January 1, 2001.

M A ᴊ ᴏ ʀ   C ᴀ ʟ ᴇ ɴ ᴅ ᴀ ʀ   R ᴇ ꜰ ᴏ ʀ ᴍ   M ᴏ ᴠ ᴇ ᴍ ᴇ ɴ ᴛ s

Two proposals for calendar reform have attracted official attention in the last century: The World Calendar, a simple change with big benefits over the current system, and The International Fixed Calendar, a 13-month design with identical lunar months. The League of Nations killed the 13-month calendar in 1937, and the US withdrew support of The World Calendar in 1955. However, the recent emergence and popularity of the new **13-Moon Calendar Change Movement** and the Mayan Dreamspell Calendar is a cultural phenomenon which has revived the lunar calendar in a more soulful, evolved, and interconnected context.

There are lots of other fascinating new reforms, such as **The Earth Calendar for the Space Era** which should be examined and considered.

THE WORLD CALENDAR
A SMALL CHANGE WITH BIG BENEFITS

Since 1930, The World Calendar Association has been advocating a simple modification to the Gregorian system with huge improvements. Their World Calendar is a perennial 12-month calendar with equal quarters, so it is reusable, sustainable, perpetual, and simple. That's right, you can use the same calendar every single year!

The current Gregorian / Julian system is an annual calendar that becomes obsolete every year. Its typical 365-day cycle is not evenly divisible by seven, the number of days in the week. One day is left over, which causes the year to always begin on the following weekday, requiring a new calendar every year. So the Gregorian system is actually a variously ordered cycle of 14 calendars—One for each new day of the week starting each New Year, and one for each leap year—a total of 14!

This 365th day boondoggle can be solved simply by removing that day from the calendar! Each New Year would typically begin on the exact same weekday as the previous year. The extracted day is declared a 24-hour "day off;" a global holiday called **World Day**, before starting each New Year. Then, if **Leap Day** is also removed and changed to another global holiday, the New Year always begins on the same weekday. These minor changes stabilize the system and create a perennial, perpetual calendar.

Every year is the same, beginning on Sunday, January 1, and each work year begins on Monday, January 2. Each month has 26 weekdays, plus Sundays. Years divide regularly into equal quarters which begin on Sunday and end on Saturday, with exactly 91 days, 13 weeks or 3 months, with 31, 30, and 30 days respectively.

Now why didn't Sosigenes think of this!

T H E   D R E A M S P E L L   C A L E N D A R
D A Y K E E P I N G   W I T H   N A T U R E   A N D   S P I R I T

The Dreamspell Calendar is a part of the prophetic time release of the ancient Maya, whose superior understanding of time and cycles provided the construction of the most accurate calendar system of any civilization. They obsessively scrutinized the heavens, aware of all the planets in the solar system, and meticulously performed their esoteric mathematics connected to the cycles of Venus and the entire galaxy. They chiseled into stone dates and times of eclipse, equinox, and solstice which 500 years later are still accurate to within a half a minute of actual occurrence! Classical Mayan dates are based on the *Long Count,* mathematically accurate to within one day over a period of 374,000 years! They also set an end date for the calendar—December 21, 2012.

This calendar provides both a physical and spiritual perspective on time. It utilizes the 28-day human female biological cycle for the physical aspect of time, because it is so closely attuned to the readily observable cycle of the moon. This sacred calendar known as the Tzolkin, has an annual cycle of 260 days made of smaller cycles of 13 and 20 days, each turning concurrently. The Maya say the spiritual cycle came to them from alignments and attunements with the frequencies of the stars of the galaxy. This spiritual cycle is then overlaid with the physical cycle to provide an accurate and holistic perspective on the unfoldment of time. Each day is galactically attuned emanating a specific meaning and resonance which expresses the beauty and power of one's full presence. This is why the Classic Maya are considered a galactic culture.

IMIX IK AKBAL KAN CHICCHAN CIMI MANIK LAMAT MULUC OC

CHUEN EB BEN IX MEN CIB CABAN ETZNAB CAUAC AHAU

T H E   M A Y A N   D A Y   S I G N S

The traditional calendar of the Maya uses three different dating systems in parallel: The Long Count, the Tzolkin, and the Haab (civil calendar). Only the Haab has a direct relationship to the length of the year.

Mayan periods have six essential parts each revolving on 13 tone sprockets.

- **Baktuns:** Periods of 144,000 days (approximately 394 years)
- **Katuns:** Periods of 7,200 days (approximately 20 years)
- **Tuns:** Periods of 360 days (18 unial), approximately a year
- **Tons:** Periods of 260 days
- **Unials:** Periods of 20 days (kin)
- **Kins:** Periods of 1 day.

A Great Cycle is 13 baktuns or 1,872,000 days (5125 years plus 134.75 Gregorian days). We are closing in on the closure of this 13th and final baktun. This end date is generating vast speculation about our current place in the space-time continuum. Is this indeed the end of time, the apocalypse, Armageddon, Ragnarok, the Rapture, or one of the many other names assigned to the monstrous final clobbering of humanity. Perhaps as I suggested in **The Grand**

Catharsis, it marks the end of one world and way of life, and the beginning of another, with the emergence of Homo Novo, the dawn of a new species on planet Earth? Or, is this simply the end of time, and the beginning of time-less-ness? Only time will tell. The Dreamspell is an accurate, vibrant system which elevates and vivifies the calendar beyond its classic function as a synchronization device into an attunement instrument. Is a massive conversion to the Mayan system possible? Let's be realistic. Best estimates find there are perhaps a million people who subscribe to this system, with less than 10% proficient enough to use it regularly. I think it is a wonderful system and I encourage everyone to become more educated and involved with it. Yet it will remain a vital subsystem like Western or Vedic astrology, but not the device by which we synchronize time on Earth.

THE WORLD THIRTEEN MOON CALENDAR CHANGE MOVEMENT

Jose Arguelles, whose breakthrough work helped decode the Mayan calendar, is the vortex of the World Thirteen Moon Calendar Change Peace Movement. He pursues the calendar's removal and replacement with revolutionary zeal: "If the human race does not reject the current twelve-month Gregorian Calendar and replace it with the new Thirteen Moon 28-Day Calendar, it will very soon bring about its own self-destruction. Changing calendars (by this date) is a planetary ultimatum."

The enigma with this "ultimatum" is that the date for the "time shift" keeps shifting: First 1992, then 1995, then 1997, now...? This movement is the spearhead of a peace plan that calls for a universal cease-fire to observe the unprecedented calendar change on July 25, the Day Out of Time, with a five-year follow-up program, Pax Cultura Pax Biospherica, as we enter the "psychozoic era."

Arguelles claims the current Gregorian Calendar and the mechanical clock constitute an artificial 12:60 timing frequency which is responsible for human alienation from nature, and the creation of a thoroughly materialistic civilization dominated by money and machines. They maintain that the impact of changing to the biologically accurate 13-Moon Dreamspell calendar will redirect humanity back into the correct timing frequency (13:20) of nature. Arguelles asserts "this is a fundamental change mandated by divine authority that transcends and unifies all sects and creeds in a higher calling of the Earth."

THE EARTH CALENDAR FOR THE SPACE ERA

There are three essential points in this calendar:

* A New Year Zero beginning on the Gregorian date of 1969—a turning point in the history of Earth when a human being took his first step on a celestial body. This event provides a reference point of great potential for cultural and scientific achievement, and future human and global evolution.

* Every day of the week and each month of the year is renamed, based on the nurturing of positive qualities of the human soul, whose rational, emotional, and universal potency provides affirmative benefits for both the individual and the community.

* Dates that indicate special astronomical events of universal importance such as solstices and equinoxes are declared holidays and subsequently celebrated.

THE LIGHTSHIFT SOLUTION FOR THE NEW MILLENNIUM

Here's my solution for a new calendar for the third millennium. The conversion from the Gregorian system to the World Calendar would be simple, sensible, and symbolic of supporting a sustainable system. It boils down to making January 1st an "un-day," which it already is in most cultures. Think how many trees could be saved and how much simpler life would be using a calendar with perpetual consistency. I would like to see this calendar implemented at the official beginning of the new millennium, January 1, 2001. Since days already have planetary derivatives for their names, I think a

Global Calendar Council should consider renaming the months to attune to and empower universal and archetypal qualities of the soul, like the Dreamspell or Earth Calendar, instead of memorializing egotistical historical personages.

Finally, at the beginning of the new millennium, 1/1/2001, I think we should reset the calendar to Zero: 1/1/2001 becomes 0/0/0000. Why? It would resolve the millennial quirk once and for all, of beginning decades, centuries and millennium's at 1 instead of 0. Zero has its roots in the Buddhist term sunyata, meaning the essence of all things, the void, the Divine Mother from whom everything is born and all returns. In the holographic cosmology of the Maya, zero is a four-petaled flower, a cyclical fountain of creation from which everything springs and eventually returns.

0/0/0000 would mark a psychological new beginning—a turnaround, a clean slate starting with zero, the circular number representing unity, infinity, and boundless possibilities for a brighter future. May the circle be unbroken. Then we can start making some real time on planet Earth.

> "To every time there is a season, and every season, a purpose under the heavens"
>
> **—Ezekiel, Ecclesiastes**

M Y   D R E A M   2 0 0 0

by Dr. Robert Muller
Chancellor of the University for Peace
Former Assistant Secretary-General of the United Nations

I Dream...

That on 1 January 2000

The whole world will stand still
In prayer, awe and gratitude
For our beautiful, heavenly Earth
And for the miracle of human life.

I Dream...

That young and old, rich and poor,
Black and white,
Peoples from North and South,
From all beliefs and cultures
Will join hands, minds and hearts
In an unprecedented, universal
Bimillennium Celebration of Life.

I Dream...

That the year 2000
Will be declared World Year of Thanksgiving
By the the United Nations.

I Dream...

That during the year 2000
Innumerable celebrations and events
Will take place all over the globe
To gauge the long hard road covered by humanity
To study our mistakes
And to plan the feats
Still to be accomplished
For the full flowering of the human race
In peace, justice and happiness.

I Dream...

That the few remaining years
To the Bimillennium
Be devoted by all humans, nations and institutions
To unparalleled thinking, action,
Inspiration, elevation, determination and love
To solve our remaining problems
And to achieve
A peaceful, united human family on Earth.

I Dream...

That the third millennium
Will be declared and made
Humanity's First Millennium of Peace.

Dr. Mueller is witnessing his prophetic dream for the year 2000 coming true. The vision of the millennial years as a launching pad for positive change has morphed and spread, as hundreds of inspired projects are taking form. The following is a small sampling of some of the visions and projects in progress.

THE APPEAL OF THE NOBEL PEACE
PRIZE LAUREATES
"FOR THE CHILDREN OF THE WORLD"

To: The Heads of States of all member states of the General Assembly of the United Nations:

Today, in every country throughout the world, there are many children silently suffering the effects and consequences of violence.

This violence takes many different forms: Between children on the streets, at school, in family life and in the community. There is physical violence, psychological violence, socio-economic violence, environmental violence and political violence. Many children—too many children live in a "culture of violence".

We wish to contribute to reduce their suffering. We believe that each child can discover, by himself, that violence is not inevitable. We can offer hope, not only to the children of the world, but to all of humanity, by beginning to create, and build, a new Culture of Non-Violence.

For this reason, we address this solemn appeal to all Heads of States, of all member countries of the General Assembly of the United nations, for the UN General Assembly to declare:

That the first decade of the new millennium, the years 2000-2010, be declared the **"Decade for a Culture of Non-Violence."**

That at the start of the decade the year 2000 be declared the **"Year of Education for Non-Violence."**

That non-violence be taught at every level in our societies during this decade, to make the children of the world aware of the real, practical meaning and benefits of non-violence in their daily lives, in order to reduce the violence, and consequent suffering, perpetrated against them and humanity in general.

Together, we can build a new culture of non-violence for humankind which will give hope to all humanity, and in particular, to the children of our world.

With deepest respect,

The Nobel Peace Prize Laureates

Signed by: Mairead Maguire Corrigan, Nelson Mandela, Mother Teresa, Aung San Suu Kyi, The 14th Dalaï Lama (Tenzin Gyatso), Mikhail Sergeyevich Gorbachev, Shimon Péres, Elie Wiesel, Mgr. Desmond Mpilo Tutu, Adolfo Pérez Esquivel, Yasser Arafat, Mgr Carlos Felipe Ximenes Belo, José Ramos-Horta, Norman Borlaug, Oscar Arias Sanchez, UNICEF, Frederik Willem de Klerk, Betty Williams, Lech Walesa, Joseph Rotblat.

THE EARTH PROCLAMATION
FROM THE EARTH RAINBOW NETWORK

We are One people...
We share One planet...
We have One common dream...
We want to live in peace...
We choose to protect and heal the Earth...
We decide to create a better world for all...
We will do our best to make that dream come true...
We will change what needs to be changed...
We will learn, to love, share and forgive...
We are One people, we want to live
and we will.

Personal Commitment
I_____

aware that human activities are seriously endangering the fragile ecosystems of our planet, aware of the widening gap between the have's and the have-nots, aware of the need to redirect my energies to protect and restore the global Web of Life, decide to begin right now to rethink my ways and values, and change what needs to be changed in myself and around me. I want the year 2000, a symbol for a New Beginning, to be the turning point in the local and global efforts now underway to create a better world based on equality, justice, and a sustainable planet, a world in which Peace on Earth prevails. Understanding that we are all individually responsible for the kind of future we will create for our children and for countless generations to come, I will participate in initiatives, locally and globally, to transform our world and protect this Jewel of Life we call Earth. I agree with this Earth Proclamation and personally commit myself to do all that I can to spread it throughout the world and help make our shared dream of Peace, Love and Harmony on Earth come true.

The Earth Rainbow Network is a growing coalition of inspired projects for the new millennium centered around the motto, "One Planet, One People, One Peace," which also intends to organize a series of large global celebrations for January 1, 2000.

THE GLOBAL PEACE CENTER

The Global Peace Foundation intends to transform Alcatraz Island, once a place of pain and suffering into a "Jewel of Light." Featuring "The One Earth One People World Cultures and Conference Center," and "The Harmonium," a hi-tech multimedia healing dome, the Global Peace Center wishes to serve as a revolutionary political metaphor for a global renaissance of enduring peace for all humanity.

THE HEALING SUMMIT AGREEMENT

WE ACKNOWLEDGE THAT ALL LIFE ON EARTH
is CREATED by UNIVERSAL INTELLIGENCE,
AND THAT OUR ROLE is TO CONSCIOUSLY COOPERATE
with THE DIVINE forces
of CREATION AND COMPASSION

WE AGREE TO CREATE, SUPPORT, AND IMPLEMENT THAT WHICH
UNIFIES, bALANCES AND HEALS THE PLANET EARTH

WE AGREE TO CREATE THAT WHICH IS REQUIRED FOR HARMONY
TO PREVAIL WITH AND bETWEEN ALL UNIQUE SPECIES,
CULTURES, RACES AND REALMS
WE, AS INDIVIDUALS, COMMIT TO bE TRUE TO THAT WHICH WE HOLD
MOST SACRED IN OUR HEARTS

WE, AS A COMMUNITY, COMMIT TO LIVE OUR INNATE
dYNAMIC VISION of WHOLENESS, MUTUAL SUPPORT,
AND EXPANSION of CONSCIOUSNESS FOR ALL bEINGS.

WE URGE THE APPLICATION of THIS AGREEMENT
IN ALL HUMAN ACTIVITY ON EARTH.

This agreement was considered and approved by the first Healing Summit in Monterey, California, October 17, 1997, sponsored by **The World Federation of Healing**

THE WORLD PEACE PRAYER SOCIETY

This group, based in New York, is devoted to two basic activities.

◆ A campaign to invite people to affirm **"May Peace Prevail on Earth"** everyday at Noon. There are presently millions of people around the world participating!

◆ The planting of Peace Poles with this affirmation inscribed in several languages. More than 100,000 Peace Poles have been placed in 160 countries! Besides their symbolic significance, the thought transmission between the obelisk shaped poles creates a form of "planetary acupuncture" for this affirmation for Peace on Earth.

MILENIO
CELEBRATING OUR HUMANITY

Milenio is an international peace conference and celebration from December 27 to January 2, 2000 in Costa Rica, supported by the United Nations University for Peace, and the Government of Costa Rica. The event will bring together world leaders, Nobel laureates, musicians, artists, spiritual leaders, grassroots organizations, and local citizens, dedicated to fostering peace, justice, and a sustainable life. These global peacemakers will gather to reflect, celebrate, heal, pray, meditate, and create together in a spirit of cooperation and love. Milenio intends to focus on "Seeking the True Meaning of Peace," by reflecting on the state of the world, defining a common vision for the future, and devising means to make this vision a reality in the new century and millennium. Milenio will recur every five years—a sort of **Olympics for Peace.**

ONE DAY IN PEACE — JANUARY 1, 2000
2000-2001 INTERNATIONAL YEAR FOR PEACE ON EARTH

What if, for one day, Saturday, January 1, 2000, all the warring parties on Earth agreed not to fire a shot for twenty-four hours? What if, also on that New Year's Day, no guns were fired on the world's television screens? And what if in the ghettos of the inner city, the brothers and sisters simply lived and let live? Why not begin the next thousand years with a single day of peace on Earth?

There are nearly 30 million soldiers in the world, and the United Nations estimates that more than 200,000 of them are children. The time has come to engineer a global truce among all people's of Earth's 192 countries. It's well within the realm of the sober realities under which we live. For if we can live peace for a day, we can live it for a week, a year....a millennium.

W O R L D   L E A D E R ' S   R E S P O N S E S   T O   T H E   P R O P O S A L   F O R   O N E   D A Y   I N   P E A C E

"In Cambodia, peace is in our minds every day, not just on one day of the year. After having suffered more than 20 years of war and devastation, Cambodian people have a longing for everlasting peace and pray for this every day. You can be sure that when you are celebrating ONE DAY IN PEACE, that all Cambodians will be praying for the same thing with you..."
- **Ly Thuch, Chief of Cabinet of His Royal Highness Samdech Krom Preah, Kingdom of Cambodia**

"The Republic of Croatia fully supports all efforts aimed at achieving peace and stability around the world, and would consider January 1, 2000 an appropriate day to commemorate such efforts."
- **Office of the President, Republic of Croatia**

"I would like to assure you that my Government and myself personally will do our utmost so that peace prevail in earth. It is my firm belief that we can all live peacefully on our globe."
- **Glafcos Clerides, President of the Republic of Cyprus**

"Activities promoting peace and mutual understanding are an active contribution to a good and peaceful future."
- **Office of the Chancellor, Germany**

"As a people we commit ourselves to making this world a happy and peaceful planet for all its inhabitants and pledge our unfailing support. We

therefore join all other countries in promoting January 1, 2000 as a day of peace, ushering the dawn of a new millennium—a millennium of peace."
◆ **Keith C. Mitchell, Prime Minister, Grenada**

"I am pleased to inform you that Guyana will observe January 1, 2000 as "World Peace Day." My government hopes that such a dedication will contribute to the process of peace in which the international community is engaged."
◆ **Samuel Hinds, President of the Republic of Guyana**

"His Excellence hopes that this laudable initiative will bring the inhabitants of the world to reflect upon their future, and that the day of January 1, 2000 will become a symbol of a new beginning for living together in brotherhood and peace."
◆ **Office of the President, Haiti**

"Allow me to express my persuasion, that the peace initiatives submitted by the organization World Peace 2000 will be successfully carried out."
◆ **Vladimir Meciar, President Slovak Republic**

"Solomon Islands is a strong believer in world peace and confirms its support to your noble endeavour and request. We agree to join other nations of the world in proclaiming 1/1/2000 as a World Peace Day in our country."
◆ **Office of the Prime Minister, Solomon Islands.**

"The Honourable Prime Minister gives his support to your efforts in declaring ONE DAY IN PEACE on January 1, 2000, as we start off the next millennium with belief and determination in achieving world peace..."
◆ **Office of the Prime Minister, Solomon Islands.**

"I fully agree and support your project for a world-wide celebration of January 1, 2000, as a day dedicated to peace...This date would be an excellent start to a hopefully more peaceful new millennium for all of us in our interconnected global community"
◆ **President Arnold Koller, Swiss Confederation**

"We are impressed by your endeavors to foster the concept of Peace on Earth and spread the One Day in Peace message. As a member of the global village, the Republic of China will continue to commit itself to world peace..."
◆ **Office of the President of Taiwan.**

"I am happy to inform you that I will be pleased to support your call for proclaiming January 1, 2000 as World Peace Day in Trinidad and Tobago."
+ **Basdeo Panday, Prime Minister, Republic of Trinidad And Tobago**

"I want to assure you of my Government's full support"
+ **Kintu Musoke, Prime Minister, The Republic of Uganda**

"Working for peace can take many forms. Protecting the environment, reaching out to people in our communities, and stopping the spread of violence and crime are all things that we can do together to improve our nation and world."
+ **Bill Clinton, President, United States**

"Zambia is committed to peace and will do everything possible to ensure the maintenance of peace and stability."
+ **Office of the President, Zambia**

"The Archbishop commends you for your efforts to promote world peace and is most willing to give his support to your campaign."
+ **Office of Archbishop Desmond Tutu, South Africa**

"I support your project World Peace 2000 firstly because peace is essential if we are to hope for a happier world in the future and secondly because every effort to achieve peace must be made by as many individuals as possible. I wish you success in your noble task. With prayers and good wishes."
+ **HH Dalai Lama**

Steve Diamond's indefatigable efforts have helped spread this "thoughtwave campaign" around the world. The following nations responded positively with letters of support for the concept of "One Day in Peace, January 1, 2000," received by Bob Silverstein of New Jersey and Chris Hildred of the United Kingdom, who spearheaded this effort.

Belgium + Cambodia + Croatia + Cyprus + CzechRepublic Germany + Grenada + Guyana + Haiti + Hungary + Jamaica Kiribati + Maldives + Slovak Republic + Solomon Islands + Swiss Confederation + Taiwan + Trinidad and Tobago + Uganda + United Kingdom + United States + Zambia

N e w   E a r t h   N e w s

New Earth News is a television program created by Scott Catamas focusing on activities and projects for empowering and enhancing life. Shows will focus on a wide spectrum of areas such as nutrition, holistic health, practical spirituality, new technologies, ecology, and cutting edge projects to elevate the quality of life.

I n t e r n a t i o n a l   C e n t e r   f o r   R e i k i   T r a i n i n g
T h e   W o r l d   P e a c e   C r y s t a l   G r i d

The World Peace Crystal Grid is made of solid copper in the shape of the heart chakra, 12 inches in diameter and plated with 24 carat gold. A 12 sided quartz pyramid is at the center under which are inscribed the Usui power symbol and the Karuna peace symbol. Double terminated quartz crystals are on each petal. Inscribed around the center are symbols for all the world's religions and the words: "May the followers of all religions and spiritual paths work together to create peace among all people on Earth."

The Grid is in a tremendously powerful location at the North Pole. All the magnetic energy of the Earth flows through this area and continues to circulate all around the Earth. This is perhaps the strongest power spot in the world! When you send healing energy to the Grid, your healing energies are sent out to circulate around the planet in a greatly amplified way. Because the purpose of the Grid is to create peace among all people on Earth, and you are one of those people, it will also send healing directly back to you.

UNITED COMMUNITIES OF SPIRIT

In a world where religious differences are too often the source of conflict, United Communities of Spirit provides a forum where people of good will from every culture, faith, and tradition can come together. UCS builds interfaith alliances, where we can learn from one another, and develop a shared understanding that can inspire and uplift the world. The explosive growth of the internet provides an opportunity for intercultural networking, our specialty for the new millennium. Here we can find our unity and common ground.

THE NEW CIVILIZATION NETWORK

The new civilization network (NCN) is a global network of people visualizaing a better world and working toward building it. A world of increased quality of life, freedom, fun, and inspiration for all. A world where the needs of all of humanity are met. One works independently or in teams on activities of your choice, cooperating and coordinating synergistic energy. Whatever your area of specialization—new energy sources, farming, education, communication, child rearing, ethics, construction, art, etc.—you simply get together with others interested in the same areas. Visit the World Transformation website to see all this in action. As NCN operational wizard Flemming Funch says, "it is time to be connected, time to collaborate, time to manifest what you are here to do, and time to bring it to the world."

WE ARE THE NEW CIVILIZATION

We are here.
We are waking up now, out of the past, to dream a bigger dream.
We are friends and equals, we are diverse and unique, and we're united for something bigger than our differences.
We believe in freedom and cooperation, abundance and harmony.
We are a culture emerging, a renaissance of the essence of humanity.
We find our own guidance, and we discern our own truth.
We go in many directions, and yet we refuse to disperse.

We have many names, we speak many languages.

We are local, we are global.

We are in all regions of the world, we're everywhere in the air.

We are universe being aware of itself, we are the wave of evolution.

We are in every child's eyes, we face the unknown with wonder and excitement.

We are messengers from the future, living in the present.

We come from silence, and we speak our truth.

We cannot be quieted, because our voice is within everyone.

We have no enemies, no boundaries can hold us.

We respect the cycles and expressions of nature, because we are nature.

We don't play to win, we play to live and learn.

We act out of inspiration, love and integrity.

We explore, we discover, we feel, and we laugh.

We are building a world that works for everyone.

We endeavor to live our lives to their fullest potential.

We are independent, self-sufficient and responsible.

We relate to each other in peace, with compassion and respect, we unite in community.

We celebrate the wholeness within and around us all.

We dance to the rhythm of creation.

We weave the threads of the new times.

We are the new civilization.

"...the God of love and peace shall be with you."
—II Corinthians 13:11

The Rites of Passage

LIGHTSHIFT 2000

9

THE HEALING OF HUMANITY

I believe that in essence, the key which unlocks the healing of humanity is found inside—in simply balancing the masculine and feminine aspects of our human nature. This divine marriage of masculine and feminine within mirrors the universe, and echoes the Hermetic principle of correspondence: "As Above, So Below." When the little boy and girl inside each of us is smiling, holding hands, and singing zip-ah-dee-doo-dah, we are engaged in the divine interplay of our wholeness, where eternal peace, love, and happiness shine just like the Sun.

The problem is, the little boy has been getting his way throughout most of human history, with the little girl living in the shadows. As we shift an age and a millennium, a new consciousness is emerging where the little girl is coming on strong, to help bring us back into balance.

As we cross the threshold of the millennial divide, humankind finds itself at a mysterious turning point on our evolutionary journey. On the one hand, our masculine dominated drive is pushing the envelope in progress and technology, and a segment of the population is reaching new levels of prosperity. On the other hand, this same force is driving us off the very edge of our own survival, where we have caused the extinction of thousands of species, and we now threaten the life of Mother Earth and ourselves. Yet in this race to face our death, we also find ourselves in a massive self transcendence or ascension, where a wonderful new energy is rising from the depths to the heights of our human nature. The divine feminine is mysteriously calling us to return to her chalice of creation where everyone has the opportunity to be nurtured into comfort and healing. The collective goddess within beckons us from her infinite well of compassion and unconditional love to heal the pain in our hearts, the hurts of nations, the wounds of the planet, the scars of the past, and live in peace, balance, and harmony. The reunion of all humanity with this forgiving and nurturing feminine side of our nature to achieve a dynamic balance of wholeness, is a work in progress and the hope of the future. We are witnessing this in the urge to reconnect with our emotions, our body, our unconscious, our intuition, our imagination; in our passionate embrace of nature, our family, our human family, our environment, and Mother Gaia. We are witnessing this in the reaction against the political and corporate exploitation of Mother Earth, and the acknowledgement of the need to live in balance and harmony, rather than in domination and control. A sacred marriage between the historically dominant though alienated masculine, and the suppressed yet emerging feminine, is a major part of our next evolutionary phase.

Humanity's passage through a potent astronomical and astrological flashpoint portal will escalate our evolution in this direction, as we open The Window into the third millennium.

THE MAGIC WINDOW
AUGUST 11, 1999 TO MAY OF 2000

For 30 years, the planetary phenomena at the end of the 20th century has fascinated me. Amidst all the frenzy of Earth change predictions over the last several decades, I have stood my ground: If there were ever a fertile period for big shifts, it would be in "The

Window. " Two celestial events of unprecedented magnitude indeed line the passageway to the third millennium: The Great August 11, 1999 **Total Solar Eclipse** and the **Grand Planetary Alignment** of early May of 2000. This period is charged with evolutionary promise as Earth frequencies elevate, though it will unfold differently in my view, than the popular literature sensationalizing pole shifts, ice ages, massive rearrangements of land masses, and other cataclysm's portray. I certainly expect a geological, psychological, and evolutionary surge at this time, though in much milder form than most doomsayer's sensationalize. **The Window is a flashpoint for LightShift:** A 9-month planetary pregnancy birthing a new cycle of momentous metamorphosis—where the Earth and humankind are born into their next turn on the evolutionary spiral.

This period has astrological/psychological and astrophysical ramifications, both of which I will illuminate and integrate. Now, I realize that astrology is a subject which divides the world, while my intent is to unify. Yet this body of knowledge, known as the **Divine Science,** has existed simultaneously, though independently, in virtually every culture and civilization, during every historical period on Earth. It has evolved into a wisdom-filled human language articulating the psyche's continuous interaction with the living forces of nature and the universe. History's material view of life and linear view of time are proving obsolete. Understanding the heart, soul, and mind of Spirit is a grander task than simply describing the body. **For in that understanding is incredible revelation, illuminating ancient mystery, as well as preparing delicious food for thought.**

THE GREAT 1999 TOTAL SOLAR ECLIPSE

From ancient times, eclipses have been considered signifcators of powerful changes ahead. Because the luminaries block each other and distort or darken the light, some eclipses take on an ominous flavor. Though there are usually four eclipses every year—two solar and two lunar—major eclipses are viewed as clear demarcations between a former cycle and a dawning new one. They are boosts of energy escalating consciousness over an evolutionary bridge.

Thirty years after the Moon Landing and Woodstock, on Wednesday, August 11, 1999, the new millennium will be signified by a Total Eclipse of the Sun of truly millennial proportions. Astrologically, this eclipse forms a powerful Grand Cross formation in all four 'gates of power,' or middle of the fixed signs—Taurus, Leo, Aquarius, and Scorpio (representing the Four Sacred Beasts; the Bull, Lion, Man, and Eagle). This directly links the energy of the aligned New Moon and Sun in opposition to Uranus, with each body squaring Mars and Jupiter. Neptune in Aquarius and Jupiter in Taurus are also in a square, though slightly out of "orb." The grand cross is an aspect of dynamism, and the fixed signs are powerful. This is one incredibly potent eclipse which opens the charged period of The Window!

The eclipse will be visible within a narrow corridor traversing the Eastern Hemisphere, with the Moon's umbral shadow beginning in the Atlantic, crossing central Europe, the Middle East, and India where it ends at sunset in the Bay of Bengal. A partial eclipse will be seen within the much broader path of the Moon's prenumbral shadow, which includes northeastern North America, all of Europe, northern Africa, and the western half of Asia.

How fascinating that this fixed polarity eclipse would focus on the Leo/Aquarius axis, just as the astrological age shifts into Aquarius. Because 13000 years ago, half way back around the 'Great Year' or galactic precessional cycle, the Earth entered the opposing Leoneon Age—often considered the time of the Great Flood, and quite possibly the last geopolar shift and secondary ice age. Many archaeo-astronomers are also dating the Great Pyramid on the Giza Plateau to this time, and feel the Great Sphinx was encoding the birth of this age in grand Leonine symbology.

SOLAR MAXIMUM 2000 AND PLANETARY ALIGNMENTS

The year 2000 arrives near a "solar maximum," that time in the 11-year sunspot cycle when there is a preponderance of solar activity—solar flares, prominences, coronal holes, an intensification of the solar wind, and an increase in the number and size of sunspots. The peaks in the sunspot cycle have indeed proven to be times of accelerated Earth change, and intensified weather. The last solar maximum around 1990 was memorialized by the vicious Loma Prieta Earthquake in San Francisco, devastating hurricanes Iniki on Kauai and Andrew in Florida, unprecedented flooding of the Mississippi River delta, the eruption of Mt. Pinatubo, among much other heightened activity. Eleven years earlier, the preceding solar maximum again coincided with the furious eruption of Mount Saint Helens, hurricane Ewa on Kauai, the most severe weather of the century in Northern California, the Midwest, and the Southern US, devastating storms throughout Europe, and a 400 percent increase in overall seismic activity on the planet.

Periods of increased solar activity also seem to be times of expansion or jumps in human consciousness. Several studies have investigated the influence of solar radiation on humans to try to understand the mechanisms involved. Research indicates that the endocrine system is affected, which in turn influences hormonal activity, including the production of the fertility hormones estrogen and progesterone, the "enlightenment hormone" serotonin, and the "timing hormone" melatonin. Altogether, a complex interaction occurs between the solar cycle and hormonal activity, which seems to affect everything from human fertility to heightened states of consciousness.

This magnified activity around solar maximum is further amplified when in synchrony with significant planetary alignments (as the last two cycles have been). Strong planetary alignments seem to increase solar tidal activity, intensifying the solar wind as the planets orbit the Sun—in a similar manner as the Moon causes tides on the Earth. Though the planets exert far less gravitational force on the Sun than the Moon exerts on the dense physical mass of the Earth—the Sun is composed of light multi-million degree exploding helium gas, which responds to far more subtle influences. In addition, the "forces" at work may not be just gravitational, but magnetic and hydrodynamic.

Whatever the precise mechanisms are, planetary alignments exacerbate solar activity by increasing the solar wind—a constant gale of atomic particles spiraling out of the Sun's magnetic field and ejecting some 3000 tons of mass at over a million miles per hour into space. Some of this mass gets caught in the Earth's ionosphere, slowing down the speed of the Earth's rotation enough to put increased stress on the tectonic plate margins, thus increasing the likelihood of earthquakes, volcanoes, and strange weather. In addition, when massive Jupiter (with a volume 1300 times the Earth's), with its 16 satellites, is part of such an alignment, the trigger mechanism seems to be set in place.

THE GRAND ALIGNMENT OF MAY 3, 2000

Indeed, by the morning of May 3, 2000, 7 planets (8 counting the ascendant)—the Sun, Moon, Mercury, Venus, Mars, Jupiter, and Saturn all align within (see illustration) a tight geocentric sector of 27 degrees of the fixed feminine Earth sign Taurus—with Jupiter right in the middle of the configuration. This describes the alignment from an Earth-centered view, which is highly significant for analyzing astrological/psychological influences on humans. From a Sun-centered or heliocentric framework, which explicates physical influences on the Sun, and in turn on the Earth, the planets still align, yet within a less severe 53 degree arc in space.

I feel The Window period will indeed be a time of accelerated Earth change, with many overdue seismic and volcanic zones releasing their stress. This is not to be feared. Hurricanes, earthquakes, floods, volcanic eruptions, and tornadoes are all part of nature's way; challenges humans have always survived. You may wish to get centered and clear on where you want to be and with whom you wish to be with. As we have witnessed from past cataclysm's, these events only serve to knit the human community closer together, as people awaken from their programmed agendas into the service of the *moment.*

THE GRAND ALIGNMENT

I have never seen a more catalytic outpouring of love as service in action as during catastrophe. In the face of adversity, true spirituality is born. Neighbors can suddenly elevate their relationship from not even knowing each other's names to living together! I also believe that these phenomena have been overblown by many sensationalists wishing to cash in on the financial formula of peddling fear. Multiply this by the advent of the millennium, and we are confronted with wild scenarios from geophysical pole shifts, to new maps which bear only vague resemblance to our current planet.

Changes in the dense mass of the physical structure of the planet are usually the last place they transpire. They manifest first in Spirit and Mind before the body. Consider Earth changes as cosmic chiropractic adjustments. This should also be a nova time for a vault in human consciousness to new levels of awareness. Our ease of passage through The Window will depend on our evolution: If we are ready, our passage will be smooth and graceful, yet if we resist change or charge forth with blind masculine drive, it may be like crashing through broken glass. Our future lives in our vision, our hearts, and our hands.

This is another reason why Spirit called for the manifestation of LightShift 2000 and the gathering of a critical mass of humanity merged in the same radiant spirit on January 1, 2000. You may have noticed that this date is almost precisely at the midpoint of the **Great Eclipse** and **Grand Alignment**! Prepared with this knowledge, the ideal human activity we can engage in is to raise the collective vibration of attunement with the unified field.

THE AWAKENING OF THE ETERNAL FEMININE

In astrology, the conjunction is the most powerful of aspects, representing a blending and magnification of the archetypal qualities of the planets involved. Since every new Moon forms a conjunction with the Sun, understanding the initiatory energy of this monthly point in the lunar cycle is a practical way to experience the conjunction. The Grand Alignment concentrates **all 7** visible or "conscious" planets in the fixed feminine Earth sign of Taurus. The key to each of our individual responses to this intensified force field will be our level of evolution or **"vibration."** For at the evolved level, this time represents a spiritual opportunity for a great evocation of the powers of the soul: A grand remembrance and awakening of the eternal feminine or goddess energy within the collective psyche of humanity. We will experience an unparalleled global metamorphosis and acceleration in human development. In this powerful portal of The Window, the divine feminine is giving birth to a New World, elevating and awakening humanity into a more advanced evolution, where the nurturing of spiritual qualities brings us back into balance with our sacred source. Taurus is ruled by the planet Venus, representing the feminine principle, the Goddess archetype, the anima, or internal creative source. In mythology, Venus was Aphrodite, goddess of love and mother of Cupid, god of love. This powerful concentration of Venusian energy during **the Grand Alignment has the potential of opening the heart of humanity and unleashing an unprecedented surge of love and light—unlike anything this planet has ever experienced!**

Every zodiacal sign has a higher and a lower evolution. The classic astrological keyword for the sign Taurus is I have, representing the Great Harvest. The higher evolution of this sign understands that the greatest possession of all is Love or Holy Spirit—the only **thing** which, in fact, *is* real. And with this gift of Great Harvest comes all its abundance—vibrant health, creativity, devotion, service, selflessness over selfishness, and the balance and alignment of personal desire with the greater good. As the past has shown, our current predicament has been caused by the indiscriminate scramble for wealth and power at the cost of the quality of human life. An evolved humanity, uplifted by this evolutionary jump, may now come together through vision, inspiration, devotion, and passion to create the channels for Spirit to flow into the world in myriads of miraculous manifestations.

As evolutionary frequencies escalate in the flashpoint of The Window, there will be critical choices for each of us during this world transition:

A choice of wisdom over ignorance, love over fear, the spiritual over the material, the big picture of Divine Order over the drama of our own little worlds. This will indeed be a catalytic period of great cleansing and global purification, with Spirit empowering us to live large and make bold and wise choices. The cocoon harboring the emerging butterfly is unraveling in order to make way for the new creation about to take flight.

A N D   T H E   W A L L S   C O M E   T U M B L I N G   D O W N

In my last book, **The Grand Catharsis,** I fully outlined the succession of planetary shifts which demarcated the transition point from the Piscean to the Aquarian age in the Spring of 1996. The movement of Uranus into the radiant air of Aquarius until 2003 from Capricorn, and Pluto into fiery truth-seeking Sagittarius until 2008 from Scorpio, were the primary planetary significators. This combination occurred only one other time in the last millennium, a time history records as **The Enlightenment.** This movement of outer planets from earth and water signs, to air and fire signs marks a lightening and brightening of unconscious energies, and mixes the alchemical formula for the awakening of humankind to enter the **True Age of Consciousness.** To my own surprise, astonishment, and delight, the Spring Equinox of 1996 found comet **Hyukatake** gleaming blue in the night skies, bringing forth the ancient Hopi prophecy of a Blue Star Kachina delineating the shifting of the ages. Precisely one year later, the amazing blazing comet **Hale-Bopp,** celebrated gloriously in the pre-dawn skies. *In my mind, this framed a bold cosmic signature for the change of the age.* In 1997, Jupiter also moved from the Earth sign Capricorn to the charged air of Aquarius, and in January / February of 1997, Jupiter and Uranus merged in a magnificent conjunction, supported by a stellium of planets in the sign of the new Aquarian period—forming a six pointed star with all the other planets.

In 1998, Neptune entered Aquarius for the first time in 165 years, where it will transit until 2012. This outer planet of the unconscious mind is attuned to galactic power and focuses on mass consciousness.

The higher evolution of Neptune is compassion, universal love and unity, and the sign Aquarius, is ruled by Uranus, the Awakener. With about two thousand religions on Earth and only one God described by most as **love**, there is much common ground to be found. This next phase promises to see many dogmatic walls come tumbling down on humanity's evolution toward universal truth and divine love, and the realization that within our diversity, we are all children of God in the family of human.

THE SHIFT OF THE AGES AND THE GALACTIC CONNECTIONS

Also in 1999, after 20 years of *'interception,'* the orbit of Pluto moves outside of Neptune's—returning to its usual, more potent position as the outermost planet in our solar system—and conduit with the rest of the galactic spiral. Many galactic linkages synchronously align to further awaken our consciousness. For at this time, Pluto conjoins the first magnitude star Antares, red heart of the scorpion, closely guarding the sacred heart center of our Milky Way galaxy.

Simultaneously, Alycone, central Sun of the Pleiades, moves over the Taurus cusp into Gemini, signaling a boost in consciousness and communication out of the ego circle into the galactic spiral. This all points to some intense final episodes of cleansing, healing, awakening, integration, and mastery, challenging the passageway through the flashpoint of The Window into the new millennium. It also appears that numerous ancient monuments and sacred sites all over the planet were specifically constructed to encode this turning of the ages in stone and activate in astronomical alignment: Stonehenge in England, Chaco Canyon in New Mexico, Callanish in Scotland, Chimney Rock in Colorado, among many others. For **with the ages changing in this potent cuspal vortex, marked by the alignment of the solstices on the same plane as our galaxy,** we are simultaneously shifting many powerful cyclical gears.

T H E   W I N D O W   2 0 1 2

Sure enough, the next solar maximum peaks during the much heralded year of the end date of the calendar of the Maya in the year 2012. End time speculation abounds around the close of this 13th and supposedly final Baktun of the Mayan calendar. The Maya were also deeply absorbed in sunspots and their relationship to Earth and consciousness changes, relating the cycles of Venus to sunspots and shifts in the magnetic field. I have seen incredible calculations tracking the Mayan **"super-numbe**r" of 1,366,560 or 20 Venusian sunspot cycles of 68,328 days, to mark a powerful and transformative solar magnetic field shift at the completion of this 26,000 year cycle in 2012. I have also witnessed amazing work in decoding the ruins of the Temple of Inspirations at Palenque, exhibiting the stellar alchemy of a magical culture leaving a message in stone of a journey of solar return in 2013. The communication of this last calendrical fractal seems to be a clear signal for us to release any fear and enter surrendered and wonder-struck to the dawn of a new solar reality. Much of the world of the past may indeed be well on its way to passing away. What crashes into ashes and rises from the remains will build the foundation of the world of tomorrow on more evolved and sacred ground. Our ability to come together as a human family will be at the very core of this transformation.

For in the language of the Tzolkin—the sacred round and harmonic module representing the infinite permutations of the universal principles of Hunab Ku, the Creator—the number 13 has a most sacred significance. In the galactic memory circuit of the Zuvuya, all things return to themselves. The number 13 is the highest heaven of the Maya, where every ending births a new beginning. By 2012, I hope to see a flourishing human culture where our children are experiencing both Heaven on Earth, and "a return path to the stars," both in the magnificent skies, and their sparkling eyes.

"The most beautiful thing we can experience is the mysterious. It is the source of all true art and science."
—Albert Einstein

2013

THE FULFILLMENT

THE EYES OF A CHILD

In grammar school in 1960, we would build crystal radios out of a few wires, a crystal, and a plastic box, and electromagnets from an iron bar, some wire, and a battery which lit up a row of lights. The Space Race was roaring, and it was a thrill seeing Russia and the US orbiting the first satellites—even if we had to crunch under our desks in drop drills each Friday morning to ear piercing air raid sirens. Many of us aspired to be astronauts, because when we grew up, we might pilot the first space ships. We would see movies of models of the clean and modern cities of the future, complete with magnetic trains, futuristic monorails, electric busses and cars, moving sidewalks, and spaceports with regularly scheduled flights to the heavenly bodies.

One of my favorite school films was called "Our Mr. Sun," which began with this astounding fact: "Energy flows from the Sun to our Earth at a constant rate of 170 billion megawatts each day— or about 25,000 times the total global energy demands." "It's simply up to us to learn how to use it." And the friendly moderator repeated a slogan throughout the movie, which continues to echo like a mantra through my consciousness:

"All the power that ever was or will be is here now!"
Though this was not very long ago, it was an era when gasoline was a quarter, candy bars were a nickel, service stations (which had bathrooms) sent a team of attendants to work on your car, and bottled water was just for steam irons. Of course, ten year olds did not care much about entrenched special interests, back room politics, lobbys, or corporate greed. When we imagined the future, it was filled with golden promise, where human genius and natural resources would unite to create a wonderful world of the future.

Now, some thirty years later, half of our children breathe unhealthy air, almost everyone must drink purified water from bottles, and we swim in polluted dying oceans. Scientists and world leaders are holding global summits to grapple with the reality that the age of fossil fuels has changed the Earth's climate to a cataclysmic condition. In the century since we began making power out of oil, we've travelled well down the road of destroying our planet.

At the beginning of the century, Nikola Tesla was generating free energy at his Wardencliffe Tower project, when JP Morgan pulled the financial plug. Free energy would stop industrial mining interests from wiring the world with copper and utilitiy companies from metering and charging for energy. Since then, trillions of dollars have indeed been made, only to reach a turning point at the dawn of the third millennium where the fossil fuel gauge approaches empty and Mother Gaia weeps in her warmed and darkened skies. Hopefully civilization will reverse this free fall and rise again.

"SOME OF THEM GREW ANGRY, by THE WAY THE EARTH WAS AbUSEd, by THE
MEN WHO TRIEd TO FORGE HER bEAUTY INTO POWER."
—JACKSON BROWNE

A   F L A S H   O F   V I S I O N

I was enjoying a vigorous workout on a stairmaster at the YMCA, when a light bulb popped on in my head. First I flashed how as a small boy I'd ride around at night on my Schwinn bike illuminated by the light of the generator which spun from my pedal power. Then I looked around and considered how if the rotating energy of all these stationary bicycles, treadmills, "spinners," stairmasters, and other apparatus were simply connected to similar generators as my Schwinn, huge amounts of electrical energy could be made. There would certainly be an excess of what the YMCA uses. And if all this energy could be stored, the thousands of kilowatts generated getting fit could light up the town.

Then I recalled the JFK physical fitness program of the early 60's in the US, and how it ignited young American's hearts toward health. Perhaps an enlightened leader of the new millennium could propose a Kilowatt Contest for the fitness facility which could generate the most energy. The fitness craze would be refueled with the greater purpose of cleaning up the environment. Or perhaps some enterprising business interest will devise retrofit devices for popular fitness apparatuses. With a little modification, our gyms could serve as human electrical power generation plants. **Let there be light!**

The formula for the renewal of our civilization seems simple: Enlightened vision must bring into alignment our resources and ingenuity around the common good. The genius of our civilization must be allowed to flourish!

The brilliance of mind—the incredible resource of human ingenuity is virtually unlimited. When unleashed and empowered, or when staring the challenge of survival straight between the eyes, it has mothered unfathomable invention. That same imagination which discovered how to split atoms and create weapons of mass destruction must now be focused on tapping clean, renewable energy for the survival of humankind and Mother Earth. The time has arrived for global citizens to adopt a **Space Race** mentality toward harnessing and using clean, sustainable energy.

"All the power that ever was or will be is right here now!"

E N E R G Y   I S   A T   T H E   H E A R T

Almost everything in our economy depends on energy. Our food, for example is planted, harvested, and transported by costly gasoline powered machines. Our cars, trucks, planes and busses, our homes, buildings, and cities; our clothing, and all our electrical devices and appliances, are all dependent on costly power from dangerous and polluting nuclear or fossil fuel powered energy. As long as we depend on these limited sources of non-renewable energy, pollution will increase, prices will rise, poverty will remain, and we will still be at the mercy of dubious overseas governments and multinational power brokers. Energy is the centerpiece and heart of the economy. Now if we can liberate energy from the shackles of control and dependence, abundance will spread and pollution will be eliminated. We live at that turning point when energy is about to become free like it flows from the Sun, the wind, the water, and the cosmos.

I ' V E   G O T   T O   A D M I T   I T ' S   G E T T I N G   B E T T E R !

In 1997, only 1% of the world's energy came from solar energy, wind turbines, water wheels, and other renewable resources, while 99% came from fossil fuels and nuclear power. But the race to liberate power is on. The use of solar and wind power is growing more than 25% a year. Just as computers replaced typewriters, and automobiles followed horses, fossil fuels will soon be history. This process must be accelerated!

In Japan, solar electric generating silicon roof tiles will cover some 70,000 homes in the next few years. 6% of Denmark's electricity is now coming from electricity generated by wind turbines. Across the German countryside, thousands of hundred-foot wind powerhouses transform wind into power for business and homes with no harm to the environment. In Europe, scores of solar office buildings generate power while transmitting filtered sunlight from their photovoltaic-laced south facing windows. Major automobile manufacturer's hybrid electric cars have hit the streets, getting twice the fuel economy while emitting half the pollution of their gasoline counterparts. As the costs go down, the roads should be ruled by non-polluting vehicles. This process must be accelerated!

As we transition from a fossil fuel to a solar hydrogen economy, much more advanced technologies dawn on our horizon. Fuel cells, born in the US Space Program, which blend hydrogen and oxygen without moving parts to create clean and quiet electricity with only clean water as waste, are being tooled by entrepreneurs to produce household units which can supply power and hot water for millions. Soon they will also be the powerplants of early 21st century automobiles.

In the US, the motor vehicle population has grown six times as fast as the human population, with about 180 million vehicles running down the road. Making inroads on these old technologies battling oil companies, political lobbies, and other entrenched interests is a veritable David and Goliath scenario. Visionary and compassionate capitalism and market demand have inspired companies like Daimlier-Benz to target making 100,000 fuel cell vehicles by 2004—up to one fifth of their fleet. Toyota has allocated almost $1 billion annually to its green machine program and is rolling out the prototypes. But the costs are still prohibitively high to compete in the marketplace. We are overdue to provide new stimuli to catalyze and empower these endeavors.

In the late '70's after the Arab oil embargo, California provided huge tax incentives for alternative energy technologies, which instantly blossomed into a thriving industry. The time has come for government to restore and enhance these incentives to overcome the inertia of a century of obsolete fossil fuel technologies. It's time for utility companies to listen to the spirit of Mother Earth and invest in renewable and sustainable alternatives. And it is time for everyone to catch the wave of the future, support environmentally correct technologies, and leave behind the dinosaurs of the past.

As GM EVI driver, actor Ted Danson exhorts, "It's sweet to be environmentally correct....what sends me over the edge is how fast and smart this car is." "This car is hot and sexy," boasts realtor Constance Chesnut. "It's a cross between a Porsche and a violin," says inventor Calvin Theobold. Why not be the first on your block to drive a clean, green machine!

FISSION OR FUSION: SEPARATION OR UNITY

The nuclear energy industry was a technology rushed into being because of the Arab oil embargo. The problem of disposing of the lethal radioactive wastes such as plutonium, which remain deadly for 50,000 years, was also overlooked, thinking science would find a solution in the future, though it never did. Nuclear fission requires that atoms be smashed in accelerators which release their energy. Fission energy is crude, polluting, limited, dangerous, and seems to violate the natural order of the universe. It must be controlled by governments or large utilitiy conglomerates, and is subject to disasters such as at Chernobyl and Three Mile Island. This splitting is symbolic of the separation or division of man from his inner source or divine connection, otherwise known as the unified field, universal, or higher Self.

The opposite of fission is fusion, which is a process of coming together or union. In Eastern tradition, the word Yoga means union, that same energy which brings us together with our source, which is love. Fusion, which creates power from subtle energy fields is safe, clean, renewable, efficient, brilliant, and virtually free.

INFINITE ENERGY FROM ZERO POINT

We live in a vast sea of infinite energy. Everything—every atom, every subatomic particle is in constant motion, spinning and vibrating eternally. In the cold dark absolute vacuum of empty space, there exists what the New Physics calls the Quantum Vacuum Flux, or Zero Point Energy. It is the ether of ancients, the prana of yogi's, the life force of metaphysics—what new science identifies as the random fluctuations of a vast field of potential in which space and time are embedded.

"A<small>NY</small> sufficiently advanced technology is indestinguishable from magic"
—A<small>RTHUR</small> C. C<small>LARKE</small>, 2001

The ghost of Nikola Tesla haunts the status quo. Like slavery in the 19th century, energy is about to be emancipated in the new millennium. Fifty years after the birth of the nuclear age, an astonishing source of energy has been discovered. Theorists cannot fully explain it, many reject it, but there is no doubt it exists. It may be far more potent that the fusion energy of the stars, and it has no known limits. It will end the world as we know it—this time, for the better!

This infinite energy source has been theoretically, mathematically, and practically proven. We are witnessing the birth of a new science and industry devoted to harnessing this force from the very fabric of space-time for practical applications. Tapping Zero Point Energy provides another free and inexhaustible resource of clean unlimited power. A scientific revolution is blossoming with thousands of tireless innovators and visionaries learning how to connect and apply this infinite energy source. As Earth's fuel gauge approaches empty in our children's and grandchildren's maturity, business interests are starting to see dollar signs in the market of setting energy free. With some funding, a free energy industry will flourish and capture the marketplace of the future. As inventor Dennis Lee exalts, "We're about to rock your world!"

S<small>HOW</small>   M<small>E</small>   <small>THE</small>   M<small>ONEY</small>!

These pioneers are not waiting around for the government or established scientists to catch this wave of the future. Dr. Eugene Mallove and his colleagues at Infinite Energy Magazine have formed an investment capital pool for Cold Fusion and New Energy called "SuperPower, Inc." They intend to link their vast technical expertise with investors and projects to accelerate the development of these new technologies into the marketplace. There are many other embryonic financial organizations in formation around the vision of capitalizing ventures devoted to personal and planetary transformation. A compassionate, open hearted capitalism embracing a passionate higher vision in a booming free market economy has great potential for brightening the future.

Now is the time to turn to the sun, the wind, the water, and the ethers for our energy. Let us empower each other to support the use of our ingenuity and natural resources. We are witnessing the birth of a sustainable global solar hydrogen economy which liberates us from the messy fuels of the past. Most modern wars have been fought over oil and energy. We can eliminate our dependency on foreign oil, create millions of new jobs, further the cause of peace, and help clean the environment simply by supporting unlimited clean electrical energy. Let there be Light!

John McConnell, the founder of Earth Day proposes the Earth Trustee Agenda: "Let every person and every institution now think and act as a responsible trustee of Earth, seeking choices in ecology, economics, and ethics that will provide a sustainable future, eliminate pollution, poverty, and violence, awaken the wonder of life and foster peaceful progress in the human adventure."

Where there is vision, the people prosper. And as the bible says, **"where there is no vision, the people perish."**

Perhaps we can dust off those grammar school models of the cities of the future. A Star of Hope shines in the new millennium skies. If we can simply align our will with the Divine Will: The beauty of the human heart, the brilliance of mind and the divinity of Spirit with a brighter new vision—we will not only survive, but thrive into a miraculous future where our children's children glow in the magic of life.

"IN THE BEGINNING, God CREATED THE HEAVEN AND EARTH
AND THE EARTH WAS WITHOUT FORM AND void
AND dARKNESS WAS UPON THE FACE OF THE dEEP,
AND THE SpiRIT OF God MOVED UPON THE FACE OF THE WATERS
AND God SAID, 'LET THERE bE LiGHT.'
AND God SAW THE LiGHT......AND iT WAS Good."

THE LIGHT PLACE TO BE

From the first burst of light and sound
The color of love began as a note
then evolved into a tone
and became a sound
a rainbow chord vibration
The sweet song of creation

Each chord a radiance
of spectral light and shimmering sound
Birthing the magnificence of life in all its myriad forms...

This infusion of light in the heavens
ignited the essence of our Heart
Each one of us a sacred part...

We are reborn
Transformed in a holy instant
At that moment
Of fusion in our essence...
In Oneness with this eternal sacred source
where all the archetypes of human experience
dance through our soul
On luminous waves of love...
For we truly are...all the love in the universe

Life is living ceremony
visual prayer
awakening insights
distant memories
deep remembrances...

The silent stirrings of sweet stillness
Awaken the flame of Mystery from the Heart of creation
Dancing dreams begin to unfold
All the mysteries will now be told

As a Golden Age is born
The True Age of Consciousness
Revealing that the Truth is the Light place to Be

Since the birth of LightShift at the beginning of 1997, thousands of people have written letters and expressed their thoughts and feelings about personal and global transformation on our website (www.lightshift.com). I am humbled to know that in the first year, several hundred thousand people are participating in the First of each Month Noon meditations from every US State and over 60 countries! You are as much the LightShift as me; it is a We thing. So I thought I'd let your words write the last chapter. Here is a sampling of some of your ideas.

As we stand at the threshold of a new millennium, it is clear that inner discoveries about the nature and capacities of the human spirit will be as important to our well-being as outer explorations on the frontiers of modern science.

◆ **Marlene Mayberry, Self Realization Fellowship, Encinitas, CA**

One individual communicating truth with conviction, is a majority.

◆ **Barrie Konicov, Tumacacori , AZ**

Let every individual and institution now think and act as a responsible trustee of Earth, seeking choices in ecology, economics and ethics that will provide a sustainable future, eliminate pollution, poverty and violence, awaken the wonder of life, and foster peaceful progress in the human adventure.'

◆ **John McConnell, Founder Earth Day, Ridgewood, NY**

Being from a culture of the Ancient Earth religions, my spirit soars to see a task of LightShift's undertaking. Spider-medicine came into place 3 years ago when Miracle the white calf was born in Janesville, Wisconsin. The elders of all Nations, the blessed who walk in light—all seem to agree on one thing. IT IS TIME for us to take responsibility for preserving what we are a part of: The Earth, and the universe. Thank you for all your effort. May each who read this and LightShift be three-fold blessed!!

◆ **Becky Beahm, Roanoke, VA**

When I became aware of Lightshift 2000, I had goosebumps all over me. I found the impetus to start such a global meditation must have come from a Divine Source. I have put the Lightshift 2000 logo on the first page of my web-page.

◆ **Bambang Pramana, Scientific Spirituality, Jakarta, Indonesia**

Every crisis is an opportunity. Let us confront the crisis of worldwide apathy, despair and violence by taking the opportunity to join hands across this great Earth on January 1, 2000 and rise together like the Phoenix from the ashes to create an active, a hopeful, a kinder civilization.

◆ **Victoria Principal, Los Angeles, CA**

When I was just a little girl, I would pray that one day all people would hold hands together around the world. I am humbled and overjoyed to see my childhood vision being fulfilled in the LightShift movement.

◆ **Oceanna, Santa Barbara, CA**

I'm a searcher from the Tropical Forest; the arm´s of the Great Mother. The Third World War won't be among nations, but among the people in its neighborhoods, and within. LightShift represents a hope and builds our faith.

◆ **Fernando Cavalcante, Rio de Janeiro, Brazil**

I am a 16 year old interested in lightwork and the global transformation of humanity in this age of light. LightShift just clicked with me! I will promote this with people at school and all those around me. Let us live our light through our love for one another and work together to bring about this change!

◆ **Ivo Visic, Johannesburg, South Africa**

I have also had a vision, since I was a child, of large groups of people participating in an activity that was felt throughout the world. I have experienced collective energy and truly believe it is the key to the transformation of the world. My appreciation for your inspiration: I will pass the LightShift word on to everyone I know.

* **Kathy Sheehy, San Diego, CA**

Only by the light of our hearts can we truly see our way into the new millenium...and only with peace in our hearts can we truly create peace in our world.

* **Rachel Smith, Makawao, Maui**

We think the secret is to unify ALL fields: All divisions, paradoxes schisms, inner conflicts. To do so takes the BIG picture, bringing together spirituality, psychology, AND cosmology, and doing the deep INNER work of purification. Light bearers have a crucial responsibility and vision for the planet at this time. May we all find stupendous ways to unify all fields!

* **Frederic Wiedemann, PhD, Unifying Fields Foundation, Meredith, CO**

I feel refreshed and inspired experiencing these pages! We can change the world and we must. I believe that we chose to live now, to live through this intense transformation, to be part of it and to help to create a new and better way—a way of coexistence and cooperation, of respect and faith, of balance and community.

* **Maria, Seattle WA**

The Lightshift is rapidly gathering momentum. Connectivity is accelerating. We are all interconnected in ways we cannot break, and in one breath, we move together.

* **Bruce Schuman, United Communities of Spirit, Santa Barbara, CA**

What did the Buddhist monk say to the hot dog vendor??? Make me One with Everything. And with LightShift, I won't need the hot dog to experience planetary unity.

* **Elaine Hendricks, Memphis, TN**

It is time to remember that Creator and Creation are not separate. You are the dream and the dreamer. Let us renegotiate the dream together.

* **Jared Rosen, Whole Life Fusion, Larkspur, California**

I am editor of the Dutch spiritual magazine Tussen Hemel en Aarde (Between Heaven and Earth). The aim of the magazine is the same as LightShift, so I would love to print your Vision as a free advertisement in the next issue of my magazine.

• **Jan Bongers, Tussen Hemel en Aarde Zaandam, The Netherlands**

I'm 50 years old and have been searching for this for along time. I BELIEVE in the power of unity in prayer and meditation. This is a good thing here, and I'm very glad I discovered this site.

• **Gale Evans**

We are our own reality; part of a universality which radiates light and beckons our participation.

• **Mary**

Here on our beautiful blue star planet Earth, we can all live in peace, harmony, and spiritual perfection. All we've gotta do is remember the words of Saints John, Paul, George and Ringo, "all you need is love," and, "let's give peace a chance."

• **Steve Diamond, Santa Barbara, CA**

The butterfly will become the symbol for a new Earth spirituality, world peace, and the new millennium with the theme of planetary transformation. It is said that the butterfly, with the flap of it's wings, can change the world and represent humanity's metamorphosis to a higher, more nurturing state.

• **Alan Moore, Butterfly Gardeners Association, Allentown, Pa**

Just a simple prayer... That all mankind realizes that we are ONE under the SUN! That we quit fighting about who is right or wrong. I pray that soon we will ALL realize in our hearts that each one of us is a perfect divine reflection of the creator. We each have an awesome piece of the puzzle to share in the grand plan.

• **Aluna Joy Yaxk'in, Mt Shasta CA**

LIVE WELL, LAUGH OFTEN, SEE THE LIGHT!!!

• **The Light Magazine, Albuquerque, NM**

I am graced and blessed to live with bear and hawk, stream and spring. I am into revering life most immediately through my devotion and honoring of Mother Earth. I am so happy to be a part of Lightshift 2000, and try to radiate light with every breath. It is an incredible time to have chosen to be here!

• **Debora Stoll, Boulder, CO**

I think that we are partly here to learn how to fall in love with Divine

Spirit all over again and rediscover the joy of being and feeling in love with God and each other. Our meditations are a trigger for people to remember the level of Light that I see approaching.

+ **Dianne, NJ**

LightShift has been called for by the ancient prophecy of many cultures. Blessings for your enlightened efforts.

+ **Alan Arkin, Los Angeles, CA**

Global transformation is dependant on our abilities at personal transformation around peaceful coexistance in this vast and rapid pace of diverse lifestyles and exchanges of information.

+ **Bill Babcock, Solana Beach, CA**

In silence we will know the truth. Let your love shine forth for all to see. What a beautiful world we can create by doing our part with thoughts of beauty and love for every living thing. Thank you for creating LightShift for those who are ready to help one another into the next dimension.

+ **Anna Beatrice, Shelton, CT**

What a TRUE Song of Joy to see humanity gearing up for 1000 years of Spirituality. Your Goals with LIGHTSHIFT 2000 echo my own......millions of people tapping into Universal Consciousness spreading Light & Love around the Globe.

+ **Rev Jack Bittler, St. Petersburg, FL**

There is the Vision, there is the Word, so let us be the Action!

+ **Ziva Bizjak, Pula, Croatia**

Thank you for your fascinating, beautiful, relaxing, curing project!

+ **Yumiko Takeda, Tokyo, Japan**

I am 70 years old, a mother and grandmother, and artist. I am very excited by Lightshift 2000. I see it as a continuation of the ideas ot Tielhard de Chardin and I am very anxious to be part of this plan.

+ **Elizabeth Brougham**

You are doing wonderful work here and I am Proud to connect with you. What a Jewel of a find!

+ **Susan Helene Clarish, Yosemite, CA**

Your project touches the hearts of gold. We are going to include your lovely material in our magazine, and will keep mentioning it until January 1, 2001! BLESS YOU for coming to this world and offering this SACRED SERVICE! Namaste

• **Dr. RA-Ja Dove, Santa Fe, NM**

I pledge my Love, my energy, and my full participation to this wondrous endeavor. I know that this Event may demonstrate a remarkable and profound global transformation on an individual level as well as in our Global Human Community. This Day serves as a Marker in Time for us to choose Peace, Wisdom, Love, and Harmony. It is our collective Destiny and the Dream awakens within us—NOW and Forever! I will spread the word and network this information among all those whose paths I touch.

• **Lynn Ferguson, McKenna, WA**

If we can get even a small number of people throughout the world to engage in the monthly meditations, it would surely have a positive effect. And if each of them gets two friends to join them, pretty soon we'll have a revolutionary movement!

• **Neil Glazer, New York, NY**

I am a lover of life, a mother, a healer, a high school teacher, a student, a child of God. Blessings for providing this wonderful focus for hope, for something positive that we can all do to help shift our direction. My hope is that more people awaken to the awareness that though we are all very different, at the core we are one light.

• **Catherine Grace, Billings, MT**

We Need This! We ARE The Circle!

• **J. Alan Rosenstein, Laguna Beach, CA**

As a long time TMer I know the value of linked consciousness. This is indeed a powerful opportunity to work together to create change. Love will indeed be all around us and will Light the Universe. LightShift is Beautiful....and Scientific!

• **Bonnie Hetherington-Robson, Ormond Beach, FL**

I think that this is a great idea. What a way to start the new millenium! We need to be as One on the Earth.

• **Nicholas Horton, Rangiora, North Canterbury, New Zealand**

My heart skips a beat while reading these pages. I am honored to share and thank my Guides for leading me here.

• **Ave marie Guenthner**

We are all light, we are all One—no one will be left behind. My spirit responded and my being filled with light as I read these pages, and the vision become mine to share.

• **Natosa, Benicia, CA**

I am pleased to learn of your project and all the meditations offered. I believe that unity in the light of spirit is the way to change this world. I am of Native American descent and am involved in the traditions of my ancestors with honor.

• **Chante Ishta**

I am a meditation master, mother, writer, Buddhist priest. We are the transformation in this moment of boundless time. Let your light shine now. The wholeness/holiness is with you.

• **Helen Jandamit**

We are dawning on a massive shift in society and the finality of the reckless abandon with which we have misused the final century of the millennium. I am happy that I see children and young people who are taking on the attitudes that people of the 60's had. Let us hope that this time people listen.

• **Lance Kelly, Townsville, Queensland , Australia**

LightShift is in perfect alignment with Divine Will.

• **Virginia Kincaid, Laguna Hills, CA**

I attended Ken Kalb's workshop at Whole Life Expo and read his book, 'The Grand Catharsis.' I have seen and heard a truly divine spirit and brilliant being with a pure heart who is living testimony. I am greatly inspired and grateful to be a part of this awesome project!

• **Wendee Lee, Pasadena, CA**

It all starts with the individual. If there is goodness in the person, there will be harmony in the home; if there is harmony in the home, there will be order in the nation, if there in order in the nation, there will be peace in the world.

• **Theresa Legge**

What a wonderful idea! We have all the possibilities in the palm of our hands!

◆ **Jennifer Lindaas**

As a Christian Mystic, Rosicrucian, and historian, I am greatly impressed with your goals. It is my desire that your aims will be met within the next century. It is attempts such as yours which will aid in creating a brave new future for all mankind.

◆ **Dr. C. E. Lindgren, Courtland, MS**

I know I have a very important job to do here in Colombia. Don't worry even if it seems a little bit violent here; there's a lot of people like me that will spend all our lives working to see us all become one.

◆ **Juan pablo Rincon, Bogota, Columbia**

Blessings for this great work; LightShift is just what we need. Our minds create our life.

◆ **Yuichiro Shida, Fukusima city, Japan**

I am thrilled and thankful to discover this most incredible website and project. I've known for years I was to participate in this event but have only now made contact.

◆ **Jody Tief**

I believe we are heading into a new era for humankind where peace, love, and dignity will flourish through individual transformation. Think globally but act locally is my motto. Love and respect your family, friends, and the people in your community, especially the elders. The Earth will be transformed magically through the power of love.

◆ **Ken Smith, Makawao, HI**

Shortly before Einstein died, he said that he wished to spend the rest of his life contemplating the nature of light. As artists of the technological revolution we now paint with light. And its essence is still a vast universe waiting to be explored.

◆ **Kimberly Brooks, Lightray Productions, Los Angeles, CA**

By expressing Unconditional love for all from the heart, we will change the world we live in. We are each as cells in the body that is planet Earth; each with a unique contribution to make to the Whole.

◆ **Peter Wallace, Love Can Heal, Cheltenham, UK**

I believe the more joy and bliss one can have in life, the more one can assist others into the light. Meditation is an important vehicle as is simply seeing others viewpoints, and dropping ALL beliefs!

✦ **Swami Virato, Publisher New Frontier Magazine, Asheville, NC**

May the Light circle the globe on that night with our hearts joined as one.

✦ **Barb & Fred Hallgrav, Phoenix Rising Unlimited, Alberta, Canada**

Global Transformation is best accomplished between the alignment of the personal and the cosmos. Astrology proves, without question, that we are connected to the universe, not isolated entities.

✦ **Henry Weingarten, The Astrologers Fund, New York, NY**

I am delighted to see so many of you here. This is a perfect example of manifesting the Spirit of what we know as God. I am deeply grateful to witness the beauty and magnificence of LightShift.

✦ **Kara Barton**

What a truly beautiful and wonderful vision. I definitely believe that we create our own realities—if we meditate and hold the Vision we will be truly Blessed to experience the Future that is our birthright. This project and all its inspirational messages resonates with me very deeply.

✦ **Crystal Foster**

Let's Light The Way Thru LOVE and Service!

✦ **Henria White Dove Smith, Wichita, KS**

I fully believe that if we all join our energies together we can transform the globe and overcome all resistance.

✦ **Mary Devlin, Winged Horse Press, El Cerrito, CA**

This project is so uplifting and refreshing. It is wonderful seeing a universal focus toward greater consciousness in effect. Thank you for your lovely work!

✦ **Nancy Cullen. Columbus, Ohio**

This is so powerful!!!!! This is so possible!!!!

✦ **Beth Delaney**

WE ARE THE World, WE ARE THE Children, WE ARE THE Ones
TO MAKE A BRIGHTER DAY, SO LET'S START LIVING.
THERE'S A CHOICE WE'RE MAKING: WE'RE SAVING OUR OWN LIVES;
IT'S TRUE WE'LL MAKE A BRIGHTER DAY, JUST YOU AND ME."

HEARTS OF COMPASSION
PUMPING WITH PASSION

My heart knows that everything is part of an unfolding Divine plan, that everything happens in its own perfect timing, and is part of a single source of all that is and ever will be. Any doubts or misunderstandings are simply from my resistance to the flow of Spirit—a current which is always present, in balance, and right in the light. I know that all of my experience is a mirror and an opportunity to demonstrate my true goodness and mastery. For each and every one of us is a masterpiece: No one can hold a candle to our unique magnificence— the core star of who we are. I know my inner world shapes my outer reality, so my happiness simply depends on the quality of my thoughts and feelings. We all have the power within to transform our lives with passion to be born to the glory of our own true self. Beyond the ups and downs, the inevitable twists and turns of fortune, let us embrace the whole of our lives in gratitude. This attitude of gratitude is the **master key** to a brighter life and a better world. Our LightShift; where our illumination, revelation, opportunity, discovery, and destiny awaken. For within each of our hearts is the treasure of joy. And as the ancient Chinese proberb affirms, **"one joy scatters a hundred griefs."**

I am thrilled to cross this threshold into the 21st century with you, and feel the mounting surge of passion in the heart of all humanity. This excitement elevates the frequency of our thoughts and emotions, igniting our collective Heart with fresh hope and deep compassion. Together we are imagineering a miracle, and the magic is abounding and astounding. We are all being born through this magnificent membrane in time: A millennium. It is our sacred destiny to be here now during this treasured moment. So let us approach each moment as if it were our first and our last. Like Jesus once said, **"the works that I do, ye shall do, and greater than I have done."** May we dig a little deeper and shine a little brighter than we ever have before. With hearts of compassion pumping with fresh passion, may the new millennium be born in the glory of love.

AXIOM	www.aloha.net / ~axiom
BrightSide TV	www.gobrightside.com
Celestial Stars	members.tripod.com / ~thirdmillennium
Creativity Cafe	creativity.net
Circles of Peace	www.boysgirls.org / co
Clinton Millennium Initiative	www.whitehouse.gov / Initiatives / Millennium
Crop Circle Connector	www.marque.demon.co.uk connector / connector.html
CyberStar Network	www.cyber-star.com
Deepak Chopra	www.randomhouse.com / chopra /
Earth Rainbow Network	www.earth-rainbow
Earth Site	www.earthsite.org
Earth Watch	www.earthsummitwatch.org /
Earth Calendar for Space Age	oasi.astu.it / Homeseudemonia / calene.htm
Earth Net Institute	207.137.115.36 / EarthNet / Default.htm
Earth Trustees	www.earthsite.org
Ed Elkin	globalvisions.org / cl / elkin
Evolutionary Ventures	www.evolutionaryventures.com
Findhorn	www.gaia.org / findhorn /
Flower of Life	www2.cruzio.com / ~flower / index.htm
Foundation of The Future	www.futurefoundation.com /
GaiaMind	www.gaiamind.org
Global Visions	globalvisions.org /
Global Solutions Nexus	www.globsol.org /
Governor's Addresses	www.worldpeace2000.org leaders / governor.htm
GreenPeace	www.greenpeace.org
Holistic Health Metabase	nodes.rhombus.net / health /
The Hope Forum	www.HopeForum.org
Human Values Project:Overview	www.uia.org / values / valcont.htm
Infinite Energy (Eugene Mallove)	www.infinite-energy.com
Inner Voice Magazine	homel.gte.net / inrvoice /
Inspire Magazine	www.mlmlionking.com index.cfm?id=051-40-7707
Jubilee 2000 Project	www.jubilee2000.org
Kidcast for Peace	creativity.net / kidcast2.html
Leader's addresses	www.peaceday.org addys.htm

Legions of Light	www.legionsoflight.com
LightShift 2000	**www.lightshift.com**
Light Party	www.lightparty.com
Light2000	light2000.com
Maharishi TM_Home.html	www.miu.edu / TM_public
Marianne Williamson	www.Marianne.com
Millennium Alliance	www.igc.apc.org / millennium / events intlsync.html
New Civilization Network:	www.worldtrans.org
New Earth News	www.newearthnews.com
Neutopia	genesis.tiac.net / neutopia
Oasis TV	www.oasistv.com
One Day In Peace	www.oneday.net
Pathways to Peace	pathwaystopeace.org
Peace Guy	www.peaceday.org
People for Peace	www.people4peace.com / welcome.htm
Project Mind (Israel)	www.webscope.com / project_mind
Sacred Earth Society	www.dalab.com / sacredearth
Sedona's Open Mind Magazine	www.sedona.net / nen / openmind /
Search For Lost Friends	www.hotbot.com
Season for Non-Violence	www.GandhiKing.com
Star Flower Essences	www.staressence.com
Surfrider Foundaiton	www.surfrider.org
Thinking Allowed TV Website	www.thinking-allowed.com
Tibet 1000 Lamp Mandala Ceremony	www.tibet.dk / charity / mandala
Tibet 2000 website	www.savetibet.org
Tom Paine Institute Philosophy	csf.colorado.edu / sustainable-justice
Tranzart	www.tranzart.com
Turner Foundation	www.turnerfoundation.org
United Communities of Spirit	origin.org / ucs.htm
University of Earth Website	www.uia.org / uiadocs / uneartha.htm
US Foundation	www.usfoundation.org
Various Earth Station	creativity.net / ccearthstn.html
Voyager (James Wanless)	www.voyagertarot.com
Wave Media	www.wavemedia.com
What On Earth Works	www.whatworksweb.comearth.html
Wisdom Channel	www.wisdomchannel.com
World Wide Servers	worldservers.org
WorldPeace 2000	www.worldpeace2000.org